A New England Town
The First Hundred Years

THE NORTON ESSAYS IN AMERICAN HISTORY

Under the general editorship of
HAROLD M. HYMAN
William P. Hobby Professor of American History
Rice University

A New England Town
The First Hundred Years

Dedham, Massachusetts, 1636–1736

Kenneth A. Lockridge

New York W·W·NORTON & COMPANY·INC·

ISBN 0 393 05381 4 Cloth Edition
ISBN 0 393 09884 2 Paper Edition

Copyright © 1970 by W. W. Norton & Company, Inc.

Library of Congress Catalog Card No. 69–14703

For Oksana,
if it's any good.

For myself,
if it isn't.

Contents

Acknowledgments

I OWE an indirect but great debt of gratitude to three French scholars whose desire to understand the rural societies of the past has opened new ways of viewing those societies: Marc Bloch, Louis Henry, and Pierre Goubert. The later work of their English counterparts Peter Laslett, E. A. Wrigley, and D. E. C. Eversley, has made possible fruitful comparisons with the English society of the seventeenth and eighteenth centuries. Special thanks are due to Lawrence Stone, who encouraged me to apply the methods of European scholars to American history, and most of all to Wesley Frank Craven, who taught me to respect the history as much as the method. Among those who have given freely of their time to help me have been Lawrence Towner; Robert Remini; Samuel Hays; Darrett Rutman; Stephen Foster; Philip Greven, Jr.; Michael Kammen; Michael Zuckerman; Edward Cook, Jr.; Jack Greene; Harold Hyman; Peter Coleman; Leo Flaherty; Patricia Feeney; and the staffs of the Woodrow Wilson National Fellowship Foundation, the Newberry Library, and the Department of History of the University of Illinois at Chicago Circle. To these, and to my wife, sincere thanks. They deserve whatever credit this book may earn, I alone bearing responsibility for its errors and shortcomings.

Evanston, Illinois March, 1969

KENNETH A. LOCKRIDGE

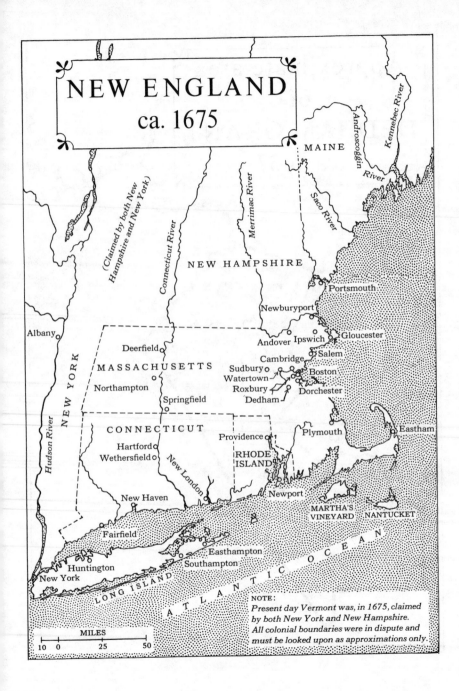

NEW ENGLAND
ca. 1675

MAINE

Kennebec River

Androscoggin River

River

Saco River

Merrimac River

Connecticut River

(Claimed by both New Hampshire and New York)

NEW HAMPSHIRE

Portsmouth

Newburyport

Albany

Deerfield

Andover Ipswich Gloucester

MASSACHUSETTS

Cambridge Salem

Sudbury Boston

NEW YORK

Northampton

Watertown

Roxbury Dorchester

Springfield

Dedham

Hudson River

CONNECTICUT

Providence Plymouth Eastham

Hartford

RHODE ISLAND

Wethersfield

New London

New Haven

Newport

MARTHA'S VINEYARD NANTUCKET

Fairfield

Easthampton

Huntington Southampton

New York

LONG ISLAND

ATLANTIC OCEAN

NOTE:
Present day Vermont was, in 1675, claimed by both New York and New Hampshire. All colonial boundaries were in dispute and must be looked upon as approximations only.

MILES

10 0   25   50

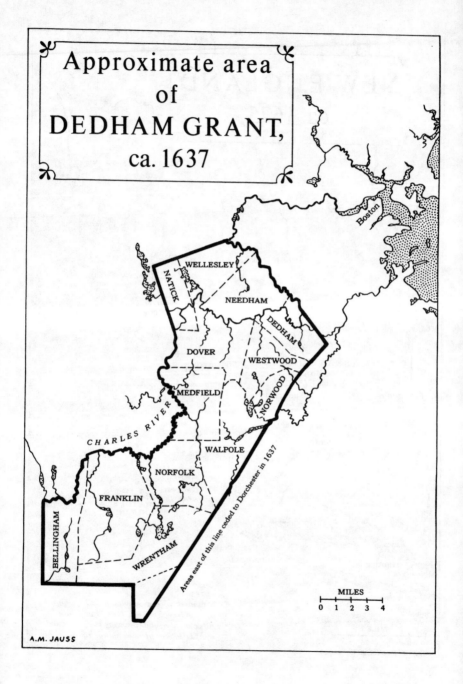

Approximate area
of
DEDHAM GRANT,
ca. 1637

Boston

WELLESLEY

NATICK

NEEDHAM

DEDHAM

DOVER

WESTWOOD

MEDFIELD

NORWOOD

CHARLES RIVER

WALPOLE

NORFOLK

FRANKLIN

BELLINGHAM

WRENTHAM

Areas east of this line ceded to Dorchester in 1637

MILES
0 1 2 3 4

A.M. JAUSS

Introduction

THE NEW ENGLAND TOWN is one of the myths out of which Americans' conception of their history has been constructed, along with such others as The Liberty Bell, George Washington, and The Frontier. In the way of all men, Americans have needed their myths. In the way of all myths, these have become true by convincing Americans that their nation has always enjoyed universal democracy, honesty, and opportunity. It would probably be a hopeless task to try to shatter any of the legendary building blocks of our popular history. And it might be pointless. People like them, a few professional historians sense various parts of the reality which lies beneath each—why not leave it at that? Why not, then, be satisfied to let The New England Town continue to evoke the responses, "democratic," "enduring," and especially, "American"?

At least in this case there are, however, reasons for trying to lessen a little the gulf between the knowledge of the superspecialized scholar and the vague popular myth. For one thing, an account of the intricate historical evolution of even a single New England town is a fine way to bring home the lesson that the past is a mixture of often contradictory events whose meaning is sometimes ambiguous. This is not a lesson that should be left for a handful of expert historians. But the New England Town commands wide attention for another reason. In its original form it embodied a way of life which prevailed both in the Old World and the New in the years when the American character first took form—the life of pre-industrial, rural, village society. As one English observer put it, this is "the world we have lost," lost in the tides of migration, mechanization, and urbanization which have since altered Western civilization.[1] It is a world which is in many respects irretrievable. It was too long ago, too different, its beliefs are too strange to be reconstructed with accuracy. Yet it is a world which made our world, in America just as much as in Europe. It was the world of William Bradford, of Jonathan Edwards, and of John Adams. We owe it the effort to understand.

Two previous layers of scholarly inquiry must be set aside in seeking an understanding of the underlying patterns of life within the New England Town. One is the basis of the myths which have so long prevailed. Both George Bancroft and Frederick Jackson Turner believed that the towns of colonial New England, together with the many settlements of the nineteenth-century frontier which adopted the same general form, had made an essential contribution to the American democratic tradition.[2] The fault of Bancroft and Turner lay not so much in the specific truth or untruth of this claim as in their tendency to point to some threads of town life while ignoring the whole social fabric; they took from the town those facts which tended to prove their point about the origins of American democracy without caring what the life of the town in its totality was or had been. The other, related layer of inquiry has dealt with the first formation of the New England Town as a study in institutional history. Where had the town, an independent and responsive institution with public meetings, elected executive board and whole panoply of locally chosen officers looking after local needs, originated? To Herbert Adams the origins lay within the customs of the tribes in the primitive German

1. Peter Laslett, *The World We Have Lost* (London, 1965).
2. George Bancroft, *History of the United States* (10 vols., Boston, 1834–1874); Frederick Jackson Turner, *The Frontier in American History* (New York, 1920).

forests. Most other scholars have passed over the Teutonic tribal gatherings, calling attention instead to the English village meetings and select vestrymen which were the obvious precedents for the New England Town. Still others have pointed out that English local institutions were modified by the settlers, abridged in the rough-and-ready conditions of New World existence into forms substantially new and distinctly American. Chief among these latter scholars has been Sumner Chilton Powell, whose *Puritan Village* is an exhaustive account of the cultural transmutations involved in the creation of a New England town.[3] Though this debate has had considerably more substance than the discussions by Bancroft and Turner, it too must be left behind in the search for the essence of life in the New England Town. Suffice it to say that the town institutions of New England were very similar to those which could be found in many villages of the mother country. The unique qualities of the New World towns manifested themselves in ways more varied and subtle than the overt modification of inherited institutions.

Having left so much behind, it may well be wondered what remains. But there is still more to be left behind. The student of the New England Town faces a difficult choice; he can either deal with many towns, asking few or shallow questions, or he can deal thoroughly with a single town, running the risk of describing an untypical example. The choice in this case has fallen on the side of portraying one town, Dedham, Massachusetts, in the years 1636–1736, though the narrative will also rest upon an unspoken knowledge of similar events in

3. Herbert B. Adams, "The Germanic Origin of New England Towns," *Johns Hopkins University Studies in Historical and Political Science*, vol. 1, (Baltimore, Md., 1882), 5–38; Sumner Chilton Powell, *Puritan Village, The Formation of a New England Town* (Middletown, Conn., 1963); some of Powell's concluding remarks overemphasize the uniqueness of the institutional framework of the New World town. Excellent general treatment of the issue will be found in George Lee Haskins, *Law and Authority in Early Massachusetts* (New York, 1962), and Anne Bush McLear, *Early New England Towns* (New York, 1908).

other towns which lends strength to its main features.[4] Taking this single community from its inception as a village of several hundred souls through the first century of its existence, as it grew into a provincial town of nearly 2000 inhabitants, makes it possible to gain a sense of the many parts of local life. It becomes possible to sense the unity of these parts and to understand the slow evolution of the whole as Dedham moved with all New England from the brief period of Puritan intensity into the long years of colonial existence preceding the American Revolution. Only from such knowledge, geographically confined but comprehensive in terms of human activity, can there emerge truly sophisticated hypotheses about all such towns, indeed about the entire history of colonial America, a society dominated by rural settlements.

The story of Dedham will be treated whenever possible within a simple narrative framework. Many techniques of social-science analysis—demography, mobility analyses, statistical breakdowns of the distribution of wealth—will inform that narrative, but as a rule they will not intrude. Greater detail might save a social scientist some trouble in reproducing the relevant calculations, but it would also burden this book with a weight of apparatus which would hobble the narrative and would be more than in this case the results, the methods, or the data justify. The book would become as much a history of the author's labors as a history of Dedham, with social scientism obscuring as much as social science has illuminated.

The main theme of the book is almost mystical in its scope. What was it like in "the world we have lost"? What was the essence of pre-industrial village life within this American town? How was this lost part of our national experience changing in the century after it began? Intertwined with this theme is another, the theme of American uniqueness. Dedham, like any of its companion towns, was a product of English culture and

---

4. Works describing other, similar towns are footnoted in the concluding chapter and discussed in the Bibliographic Essay.

an agricultural community whose basic traits it shared with villages all over Europe. At the same time, as a settlement in the wilderness and a refuge for a group of English Puritans whose very flight made them unusual, Dedham was peculiarly American. An attempt to discover precisely what was and what was not "American" in the experience of this town can sharpen the perception of the earliest sources of our national character. With these themes, incorporated into them, will be provocative or controversial questions about life in a New England town, not all of them answerable but all deserving to be asked: was it democratic, was it equalitarian, was opportunity great, was the society mobile, was it static or dynamic, who had power, who wanted power? In the end, a consideration of all these matters in the context of events in other towns will open the possibility of a reinterpretation of our rural heritage, which though America is now a thoroughly urbanized nation, is still influencing our lives—and not always in the ways we might wish.

I

A Utopian Commune, 1636–1686

In the first decades of its existence Dedham was a remarkably stable agricultural community. It was also a utopian experiment, hardly less so than the famous Amana, Oneida, and Brook Farm experiments of the nineteenth century. The founders of this community set out to construct a unified social organism in which the whole would be more than the sum of the parts. To a considerable degree, they succeeded.

1

The Policies of Perfection: The Town

~~~~~~

SCATTERED AMONG the first waves of the Puritan exodus, they had arrived in the Massachusetts Bay colony in the years between 1630 and 1635. Many of them still strangers to one another, they had taken up temporary residence in several of the earliest settlements along the shores of the Bay. Sheer circumstance helped draw them together: it happened that most of them had found refuge in Watertown, where scores of immigrants were crowding in upon one another and where much of the best land had already been parceled out to the first arrivals.[1] Yet behind the pressure of circumstance lay motives common to most of the Puritan immigrants. Within the limits set by the emerging policies of the colony, groups of settlers everywhere were coalescing and searching for the opportunity to create a communal life, seeking to shape in their own agricultural villages their own versions of the good society. So it was with the men who were to found the town of Dedham.

In 1635 they petitioned the General Court of the colony for a grant of land for a "plantation" south of Watertown. In polite phrases the petitioners asked for full control of the distribution of such lands as might be granted them, for exemption from taxes during the next four years, and for immunity from military obligations except in dire emergencies. Though the

1. *Early Records of the Town of Dedham* (6 vols., Dedham, Mass., 1886–1936) [hereafter, *Records*], II, *Church and Cemetery, 1638–1845,* 1; *Watertown Records* (4 vols., Watertown, Mass., 1894 and 1900; Boston, Mass., 1904 and 1906), I, part 2; *Land Grants and Possessions,* 1–67.

advice of the Court was solicited, the petition carried the implication that "the well ordering of . . . our society according to the best rule" would be left largely to the petitioners themselves. Significantly, the name which the founders would have given their plantation was "Contentment." Prosaic minds in the General Court changed "Contentment" to "Dedham," but the substance of the petition was granted.[2]

Late in the summer of 1636 about thirty families excised from the broad ranks of the English middle classes, coming from the towns and villages of several regions,[3] found themselves in possession of nearly 200 square miles of American wilderness. The hilly, rocky tract stretched from the southwestern boundary of Boston down to what was to become the Rhode Island border. Except for several score Indians, who were quickly persuaded to relinquish their claims for a small sum, the area was free of human habitation. Since Adam awoke in Paradise there had been no moments in which mankind had been given a clean slate, but the founders of Dedham came as close as men had ever come. They brought to their task the inevitable cultural baggage of Englishmen: language, rank, religion. They were subject to the broad guidance of the General Court. The rest, how they chose to organize what was in the most immediate sense *their* town, was up to them.

The way in which they began demonstrates the coherent social vision which had prompted this collection of men to seek their own community:

"One: We whose names are here unto subscribed do, in the fear and reverence of our Almighty God, mutually and severally promise amongst ourselves and each other to profess and practice one truth according to that most perfect rule, the

---

2. *Records,* III, *Town and Selectmen, 1636–1659,* 1.
3. The origins of some of the settlers may be traced through references in the standard genealogical works, many of which are cited below in specific contexts. They came chiefly from the North Country (Yorkshire, chiefly) or from East Anglia. See also *Records,* II, 1.

foundation whereof is everlasting love." [4] This was the first clause of the Dedham Covenant, a document in which the founders of the town simultaneously set forth their social ideal, outlined the policies by which they would attempt to bring that ideal to reality, and pledged themselves to obey those policies. Every future townsman would be expected to signify his acceptance of its terms by signing his name beneath those of the founders. The Covenant began by binding every man to each of his fellows before God in a pledge to practice Christian love in their daily lives. The unity of men living according to this "one truth and most perfect rule" was to be the bedrock of the intended community. In four more clauses the Covenant further articulated the founders' vision of social perfection.

"*Two:* That we shall by all means labor to keep off from us all such as are contrary minded, and receive only such unto us as may be probably of one heart with us, [and such] as that we either know or may well and truly be informed to walk in a peaceable conversation with all meekness of spirit, [this] for the edification of each other in the knowledge and faith of the Lord Jesus, and the mutual encouragement unto all temporal comforts in all things, seeking the good of each other, out of which may be derived true peace." They expected that all townsmen would begin as humble seekers after that true faith in the Lord Jesus out of which came the capacity for genuine Christian love. All would go together in their search for faith and would be united by the mutual love that would arise in the course of the search and would reach its culmination in their achieved faith. A deep and abiding peace within each man and pervading the whole community would be the fruit of their companionship in this course. But in such a community there could be no place for the contrary minded or the proud of spirit. These would be warned off or, if need

4. This and the following quotations are from *Records*, III, 2–3. The explications of each clause are based on an understanding of later events and expressions, as well as on the text of the Covenant itself.

be, expelled. The founders saw no contradiction in the idea
that the ideal society was to be built upon a policy of rigid
exclusiveness.

"*Three:* That if at any time differences shall rise between
parties of our said town, that then such party or parties shall
presently refer all such differences unto some one, two, or
three others of our said society to be fully accorded and determined without any further delay, if it possibly may be."
The founders were striving for social perfection, but they were
realistic about the means leading to its achievement. Even
among the most carefully selected human material there would
be some men who would now and then in the course of the
common search for faith forget their pledges and quarrel.
Indeed, there would be men who for all their trying would
never achieve a valid Christian faith. Damned by eternally
flawed natures unredeemed by God's grace, time and time again
they would disrupt the harmony of the community. So the
founders wrote into the Covenant a secular policy designed to
achieve from without what Christian love would in most cases
guarantee from within. This was that all men should promise
to submit their "differences," as they so delicately put it, to
a gentle mediation by several of their fellows. A little sincere
persuasion would remind the disputing parties of their obligations and restore the community, if not their souls, to unity
and to peace.

"*Four:* That every man that . . . shall have lots [land] in
our said town shall pay his share in all such . . . charges as
shall be imposed on him . . ., as also become freely subject
unto all such orders and constitutions as shall be . . . made
now or at any time hereafter from this day forward, as well
for loving and comfortable society in our said town as also for
the prosperous and thriving condition of our said fellowship,
especially respecting the fear of God, in which we desire to
begin and continue whatsoever we shall by his loving favor take
into hand." Implied in this clause was the assumption that

the ideal community was to be characterized by more than a vague atmosphere of peace and unity generated by Christian love and further preserved by local mediation. "Orders and constitutions" would be made to arrange the practical details of life so as to ensure a comfortable and thriving society. Pleasing to the men who lived therein, such a society would also be pleasing to a God who reserved his special wrath for disorderly communities. Accordingly, a free but strict obedience to the policies which would provide this good order was the final promise exacted of each townsman. Continuing dissent and debate were not to be permitted; once a policy was established, all men were to accept it without reservation.

"Five: And for the better manifestation of our true resolution herein, every man so received [into the town is] to subscribe hereunto his name, thereby obliging both himself and his successors after him for ever, as we have done." It was more than a lifetime contract which the founders intended; it was a contract in perpetuity, binding posterity in a continuing testimony to the hunger for social perfection which had seized a handful of Englishmen in the midst of a wilderness.

They meant what they said. The story of Dedham through the first decades of its existence is above all the story of the implementation of the policies of perfection written into the Covenant. Because true Christian love could only grow within each man's soul, perhaps with the help of the church, the leaders of secular society could do little to nourish this element of the covenential ideal. But they could and did follow the guidance of the Covenant in excluding those who would disrupt Christian unity, mediating the disputes of those who broke the peace, and instituting and obeying countless ordinances which brought every area of life into a stable secular order. Thus the promises of the Covenant were kept and there emerged a community that realized the vision of the founders.

* * *

In practice, the communal ideal was static. Suitable men would be culled from among the applicants and the rest refused. When enough men had been accepted, the community would be declared complete. The select group of townsmen and their perpetually committed descendants would then live under the rules of the Covenant, the land theirs to assign, their rare disputes contained within the town. The culling began at the first meeting, on the 18th of August, 1636, when it was agreed by all that a townsman signing the Covenant incurred an obligation to tell whatever he might know about future candidates for admission. Every candidate would undergo a public inquisition in which his entire past could be brought to light. The discovery of a lie would be grounds for instant exclusion. As admissions went forward, the townsmen moved to plug a loophole through which unexamined persons might enter. After November of 1636 a member of the town could not sell or rent for more than a year any of his land unless the prospective customer was already a member of the town or had been approved by a majority of "the whole Company." If the rule were broken, the land in question could be confiscated.[5]

An unsettled issue facing the town was that of the exact number to be included in their planned community. While the principles of the Covenant could be extended to justify a limitation on the numbers of townsmen, neither in the Covenant nor in the record of the early meetings had an official limit been set down. A temporary halt on admissions was imposed in 1637, when the first set of forty-six house lots had been assigned: "We do now therefore fully agree by a general consent that no more lots shall be granted out [or persons admitted] until a further view be made what accommodations may be found for comfortable entertainment of others . . . for we

5. *Records*, III, 20, 24; Admissions and alienations were still being controlled thirty years later; *Records*, IV, *Town and Selectmen, 1659–1673*, 205, 194.

have as many as we conceive can yet be entertained." [6] But admissions soon resumed, no official decision was made as to the ultimate number which could be "comfortably entertained," and the issue loomed larger with each new admission.

Raw self-interest finally forced a decision. The ever-increasing numbers of townsmen were diluting the land rights of the first settlers. In 1636, the thirty signers of the Covenant had shared the possession of the immense quantities of land possessed by the town by virtue of the General Court's approval of their petition. By 1637 the number of signers was forty-six; by early 1656 more than seventy-five had signed. Thus, a man admitted to the community in 1636 had shared to the rough extent of one-thirtieth each time a section of the town's land was subdivided, while by 1656 his proportion was closer to a seventy-fifth. And of course his implied share in the huge areas of land yet undivided was correspondingly reduced. Partially because of the resultant pressure from some of the old settlers and partially because it had been intended all along, the town acted to limit its growth. As of the end of 1656 the seventy-nine men then officially members of the town were constituted the proprietors of the public lands of Dedham, their shares of the proprietorship varying according to certain guidelines. Henceforth only these men, their heirs, or approved newcomers who purchased some of their proprietary rights would be entitled to join in the periodic divisions of land. While in theory strangers could, and in practice a few did, still gain admission to the town, an admission which no longer carried with it an automatic share in the town lands was not as desirable a privilege. The net effect was to set a seal to the society embraced by the Covenant.

The town had probably not allowed itself to expand very much beyond its founders' general expectations. Henry Phillips and others of the first settlers complained in 1656 that "in the

6. *Records,* III, 34–35.

infancy of this plantation . . . the first planters agreed that they would entertain only sixty persons to the privilege . . . of divisions . . . in the town commons." [7] Phillips and his friends considered the difference between the hypothetical sixty and the actual seventy-nine proprietors of 1656 to represent a harmful dilution of their rights, yet the town had come fairly close to the number forseen in the informal agreement to which Phillips referred. (As for the complainants, the town later enlarged their shares in the proprietorship, thereby easing the tension which had arisen and remaining true to the policies of the Covenant.)

Land was the ultimate reward in a society based on agriculture. Enjoying a free hand in its distribution, Dedham was able to use its periodic allotments of land to shape as well as to limit the ideal society which was to be created from its select human material. The goals which governed the distribution of land followed from the mood of the Covenant—community and above all order.

One of the standards determining the amount of land a man received from the town was the number of persons in his household.[8] Thus, mere existence within the commune gave even the youngest infant or most feeble maiden aunt a claim to its support. Another standard was "usefulness either in Church or Commonwealth," a standard which meant for the most part service to the local community, since only a handful of Dedham men achieved prominence in the affairs of the colony. Grants of land for the support of the church and a school likewise bore witness to the mutual needs of the townsmen. Every person within the embrace of the Covenant had a right to live, and to live in a community well served by its leaders and in which the suppliers of spiritual and intellectual fare were well supported. The allotment of land sustained these communal rights.

The mutuality preached in the Covenant and thus practiced

7. *Records,* III, 142–46; IV, 230.
8. The guidelines are in *Records,* III, 92.

notwithstanding, a clearly defined social hierarchy was also a part of the ideal of the founders, and the town's land policies were set accordingly. For Christian love toward all men does not have to imply absolute human equality, and in fact this particular Christian commune was not about to practice Christian Communism. To the contrary, the men of Dedham held fast to the belief of their Puritan culture in the natural inequality of men. It was foreordained by God that some men should have both greater capabilities and virtues than others and should rise and prosper. It was equally fated that some men should be incompetents and sinners who would lag behind the rest. Nor was this without its social purpose, since obedience to men of high rank was the cement of an orderly society, while the needs of less fortunate souls kept men attentive to their duties of Christian charity. Thus, the settlers did not see any necessary contradiction between their emphasis on mutuality to the point of a form of collectivism, and a frank recognition that a certain hierarchy of wealth and status was as desirable as it was inevitable, for in the view of their culture each tended in its own way to ensure social harmony. As long as within the levels of society the gap between the high and the low was not too extreme, as long as men of rank acquitted themselves responsibly and with a proper modesty, and as long as the lower ranks freely respected the upper, hierarchy was expected to add to collectivism yet another source of harmony, not to detract from it.[9]

Hence, ever attentive to the will of God and to the ad-

---

9. As will be seen (in chapters 2, 3, and 4), the conditions required for the successful blending of hierarchy with collectivism could be found in Dedham for quite some time after the founding of the town. The tensions implicit in this delicately balanced blend of opposite social ideals were as typical of Puritan social theory as of their renowned theology: see John Winthrop, "A Modell of Christian Charity," most readily available in Perry Miller and Thomas H. Johnson, eds., *The Puritans* (2 vols., New York, 1963), I, 195–99; and see Stephen Foster, "The Puritan Social Ethic: Class and Calling in the First Hundred Years of Settlement in New England," Ph.D. dissertation, Yale University, 1966.

vantages of social harmony, the founders of Dedham made "men's rank and quality" major criteria for the assignment of land. Though few if any of the settlers affected much "rank and quality" as an English courtier would have defined these, there were among them men who had been relatively wealthy or somewhat prominent in the localities from whence they came. These men received larger portions of each division of land, while men without such distinctions had to show large families or accept the smaller allotments appropriate to their lesser stations. Those who had, got, because in the Puritan lexicon those who had, deserved; and by this light Dedham acted in yet another way to perfect itself as it saw perfection.

The juxtaposition of a small band of Englishmen and a huge tract of wilderness was one of the most striking characteristics of early Dedham, but even more striking was the reaction of these Englishmen to the prospect of hundreds of thousands of acres of virgin land. Far from indulging appetites long held in check by the scarcity of land in England, the Dedham settlers' initial reaction was to turn their backs on the wilderness. During the first twenty years they divided among themselves less than 3,000 acres. They deliberately refused to indulge in the rapid assignment of large individual farms which had taken place in Watertown. Instead they parceled out to each man tiny houselots, with additional strips of arable, meadow and woodland scattered around the village. Each strip ranged from two to twelve acres, depending on the size of a man's family, his usefulness and rank; each was located in a large field in which every man had a similar strip of land and in which the common decisions of the group were to determine what crop would be sown in the field, its care and harvesting.[10] The slow process of allotment enabled the town to enforce its social priorities with precision, while the common fields brought

10. For the details of the land system see *Records,* III.

men into continual contact with one another and kept the village from disintegrating into isolated farms out in the countryside. Slowly, as ever larger areas of the common land were divided, as individual holdings were bought and sold and thereby consolidated into farms, the rigid pattern was to dissolve. Until it did, the village remained a cohesive social organism.

The overriding message of the Covenant had been simply love. Love, forbearance, cooperation, peace . . . these were the essential qualities of the perfect society whose image had inspired the Covenant. Exclusion and orderly planning alone could not make that vision real. The townsmen did not neglect the message. In the first place, they did not neglect to make use of the mediators whose advice the Covenant obliged them to seek when differences arose. There came into existence in the town an ephemeral but effective system of mediation which largely supplanted the hierarchy of formal courts established by the colony. "Three understanding men" were to determine just compensation in a land case. On another occasion, "two judicious men" were to be chosen. Damages done by runaway swine were assessed by "three indifferent neighbors" of the offending party. When Joseph Kingsbury, Joshua Fisher, and Lambert Chinnery disagreed with the town over the pre-emption of their land for a highway, each of the four parties selected a mediator while a fifth was approved "by joint consent of all parties." The decisions of the mediators (or arbitrators as they were sometimes called) were seldom challenged. Though decisions were entered in a book kept especially for the purpose so that all might refer to them as to the written law, the underlying law applied by the mediators was nothing more than the Golden Rule. The parties to a difference were urged to "live together in a way of neighborly love and do each other as they would have the other do themselves." [11]

11. *Records,* III, 24, 38, 43, 114–15; IV, 15, 118–19.

The same system governed Dedham's disputes with neighboring towns. When a disagreement between the town and Medfield arose in 1651, Dedham instructed its emissaries, "if it cannot be satisfactorily composed betwixt our bretheren of Medfield and ourselves, we shall yield to a free and indifferent reference and engage to make their conclusion good." Representatives sent to negotiate a dispute with Dorchester the next year were empowered "to conclude the case either by arbitration, composition or any other peaceable way." The instructions continued, "in case . . . they satisfy you that the title [to the disputed land] is truly and legally theirs, then you shall forbear making further claim thereof . . . [further] you shall by all your care and diligence waive and avoid, so much as in you lay, all occasions whatsoever [that] may tend to provocation or breach of peace, and shall . . . present them with the loving respect our town in general bears towards them." [12]

As the instructions to the representatives sent to Dorchester indicate, the emphasis on informal accommodation as the key to peace went beyond the appointment of mediators. Within the town as well as without, the greatest care was exercised to prevent disputes before they arose. Was the town going to pre-empt a man's farmland along the river for a mill? Then policy required satisfactory compensation, satisfactory to the owner as well as to the town. Was there bad soil in part of the next field to be divided among the townsmen? Then the lots which included bad soil would be larger than the others, so that no man could complain of injustice. Had a man not heard of the latest order forbidding the cutting of oak trees? Very well, then, he would not pay a fine for the oaks he had felled in his ignorance.

Year in and year out the keeper of the town book recorded many such small examples of solicitude. The Covenant was kept in spirit as well as in letter, and the keeping of the spirit

12. *Records,* III, 197, 208–09.

of the Covenant kept the peace in Dedham. In the fifty years after its foundation the town was entirely free of the prolonged disputes which racked some towns nearby.[13]

Supplementing Dedham's policies of perfection were lesser policies which helped maintain the social fabric. Many were policies not uncommon in the villages of England and most were required of all towns by the General Court of Massachusetts.[14] The town made its own formal bylaws, which served to protect the common interest, as in the case of laws for the conservation of timber and laws regulating the operation of the grist mills.[15] Poor persons were aided if they were members of a townsman's family, otherwise sent packing no matter how hungry they might be; the town would take care of its own but would not risk expense or scandal by entertaining impoverished outsiders.[16] The town was empowered to inquire into private lives, ordering amendment where amendment was due, putting the offender under the supervision of an upright townsman if he did not mend his ways. Thus, "upon information that John Littlefield . . . runs up and down misspending his time, and by that means may not only bring ruin to himself but also charge and damage may come to the town thereby, the selectmen . . . have ordered him to dwell with Thomas Aldridge two, three, or four weeks," and, "the selectmen having treated John McIntosh concerning the state of his family and of some . . . disorder that they understood to be in the same, . . . understanding that disorder in the family do rather in-

13. Which is not to say that the town was without its brief disputes. The above-mentioned complaint of some old settlers (led by Henry Phillips) over the dilution of their land rights, beginning in 1656, was one such; a political clash in 1660 was another, as will be seen. The extent to which these episodes undermined the ideal of the Covenant will be considered in chapter 5.

14. For examples, see *Records of the Governor and Company of Massachusetts Bay in New England* (5 vols., Boston, Mass., 1853–1854), II, 4, 6–9, 163, 180.

15. *Records*, III, 177; IV, 155.

16. *Records*, III, 196, is an exception.

crease, . . . think it meet to dispose of one of his sons to
service with . . . Timothy Dwight." The selectmen, chief
officers of the town, were also charged with arranging the
seating in the meetinghouse according to the rank of the
persons within the society. The local hierarchy of age, service,
and estate was literally displayed before the eyes of each inhabitant as he took his seat on Sunday mornings.[17] The Dedham
school, kept in accordance with the law, offered the education
in obedience and social conformity usual in the schools of the
time.[18] Beyond the local taxes all men had to pay, every man
owed the community a certain share of his time. He labored
several days each month on the roads of the town or he paid
the cash equivalent of his labor.[19] The communal obligation
extended to the myriad tedious offices which had to be filled.
Every townsman experienced days of annoyance and missed
meals while serving as constable, assessor, clerk, surveyor,
fenceviewer, poundkeeper, woodreeve, or (for the unfortunate
few) hogreeve.

* * *

Out of their vision of society and out of the wilderness tract
with which they had begun the founders of Dedham had created
what might best be described as a Christian Utopian Closed
Corporate Community. Christian because they saw Christian
love as the force which would most completely unite their
community. Utopian because theirs was a highly conscious
attempt to build the most perfect possible community, as
perfectly united, perfectly at peace, and perfectly ordered as
man could arrange. Closed because its membership was selected
while outsiders were treated with suspicion or rejected altogether.

17. *Records,* V, 111–12, 114; III, 148.
18. Bernard Bailyn, *Education in the Forming of American Society*
(New York, 1960); *Records,* III, IV, indexes under "school."
19. *Records,* V, 60–61, for one example.

And Corporate because the commune demanded the loyalty of its members, offering in exchange privileges which could be obtained only through membership, not the least of which were peace and good order. The corporative nature of the town was confirmed by the practices of the colony: the typical inhabitant of Massachusetts could obtain land only by belonging to a particular town, since the allotment of most of the land in settled areas had been delegated to the towns by the General Court; and a man was represented in the House of Deputies (the lower house of the General Court) only if he was a member of a town, since representatives were elected from the town corporations rather than from electoral districts containing a certain number of inhabitants.

The obvious origin of the Christian Utopian Closed Corporate Community lay in the Puritan ideology. The very term "Puritan" was coined to describe the desire for perfection which drove many of these otherwise typical Englishmen into martyrdom or exile. Purity in the church itself was the chief goal. The Puritans sought an end to bishops, vestments, ritual —to "papistry" in whatever form it might take. Their consciences required a return to the simple forms of primitive Christianity and a ministry which would preach the unadorned Word of God as it appeared in the Bible. What has often been passed over, however, is the intensity of the drive for social purity which likewise characterized Puritanism. If the Puritan sometimes dreamed of a church whose membership was confined to "visible saints," he also dreamed on occasion of a society dominated by secular saints, men able to live in harmony with their fellowmen as God had commanded.

Most immediately, the policies of perfection in Dedham were the products of a vivid utopian spirit which came to possess most of the leaders and many of the rank and file of the Puritan emigration as they approached America. They were aware that a great opportunity awaited them in the confrontation of the Puritan social ideal with the New World. Here was a chance to begin again, leaving behind the compromises of an established culture. Governor John Winthrop's famous "Modell of Christian Charity," a sermon delivered aboard the *Arabella* on the way to America, is proof of the excitement and trepidation with which he approached the unique opportunity opened to his people. With God's help they would build in their colony a "city upon a hill" which would stand as a shining example to all men. The plan of the society Winthrop hoped to construct in Massachusetts was the plan of early Dedham writ large, a holy covenanted corporation mixing mutuality with hierarchy and Christian love with exclusiveness.[20]

But the origins of the Dedham commune ran deeper than the Puritan ideology, deeper even than Christianity. At first glance they seem to run back to the English rural culture which had done so much to shape the social ideals of Puritanism. Any number of institutions and customs found in Dedham were direct transplantations from the English villages of the time. Genuine as this line of descent is, it is also deceptive. For the deepest secular origins of this Utopian Closed Corporate Community lay not merely in English villages but in a major strain of peasant culture also found in medieval and modern villages of France and Spain, and in modern Indian and Javanese villages.

An anthropologist entirely unaware of the internal structure of the New England Town has described the "Closed Corporate Peasant Community" common to all these places and times. His description fits Dedham nicely. Social relationships in these rural communities are "many-stranded and polyadic"; the villagers tend to form a single social coalition which deals with all the issues of village life—land, taxation, regulation, morality. A "Closed Corporate Peasant Community" restricts its member-

---

20. Edmund S. Morgan, *Visible Saints, The History of a Puritan Idea* (New York, 1963), and Stephen Foster, "The Puritan Social Ethic," will serve as background. Again, "A Modell of Christian Charity" is in Miller and Johnson, *The Puritans,* I.

ship, retains ultimate authority over the alienation of land, seeks to guarantee its members equal access to resources, and maintains its internal order by enforcing common standards of behavior (by accusations of witchcraft, if all else fails). "The community thus acquires the form of a corporation, an enduring organization of rights and duties held by a stable membership; and it will tend to fight off changes and innovations as potential threats to the internal order that it strives to maintain." Indeed, the constant possibility of disruptions imposed by outside forces generates a powerful hostility toward everything strange, a hostility which further protects the internal order by uniting the villagers in a shared emotional experience. Conscious utopianism may be found in these as in all peasant communities, for from them arise movements centering on a "myth of a social order," looking forward to "the establishment of a new order on earth." [21]

So the utopia of the Puritan émigrés who founded Dedham was in many respects a peasant utopia. [22] The communal ideal of these men repeated so many features of the peasant ideal that their Puritanism seemed a mere continuation of the peasant ethos. [23] The dichotomy of mutual devotion within and hostility

21. Eric Wolf, *Peasants* (Englewood Cliffs, N.J., 1966), 84ff., 106ff.; the quotations are from pp. 86 and 106.

22. Only an historian limited by a preoccupation with medieval European peasant society (and indeed by a narrow view of that slice of human experience) would insist that tenancy on the lands of a lord is a necessary characteristic of a peasant community. The more universal definition used by anthropologists does not require a lord or lords, since it defines as "peasant" any more or less self-shaping community of men on the land in a pre-modern context which tends to view and organize itself according to certain patterns. Landlordism merely introduces variations, sometimes quite minor ones, in these patterns. But even if the term "peasant" *is* to be restricted to European villages and/or to villages with lords of the manor, the fact remains that Dedham shaped itself in a form common to many communities of men on the land all over the world in many ages, and in this sense was part of a tradition that went beyond Puritanism, call it what you will.

23. Of the writers on Puritan New England, Perry Miller has best

without, which had been practiced by a multitude of villages all over the world for thousands of years, was in turn both preached and practiced in Puritan Dedham, and all the characteristic implications of this corporative form were worked out in full detail. Further, the tendency of medieval peasants to look on the villages of an imaginary golden past as their model for the future regeneration of society was repeated in the Puritan idealization of the communes of the primitive Christian church and in the use of these communes as a model for some features of Dedham's organization.[24] Precedents for the peculiar mixture of hierarchy with collectivism manifested in Puritan Dedham could even be found in the history of peasant utopianism.[25] The Puritan source did not simply echo the peasant; they were directly linked. The social ethic of Englishmen of the day still owed much to the peasant experience which had once dominated the English scene, and among the Puritans as among all Englishmen were many men whose families were only a few generations removed from villeinage and still lived in hamlets that were essentially peasant.

Did this really mean that for the men of Dedham Puritanism was nothing more than the continuation of traditional impulses? Not entirely. Puritanism was above all a new religious impulse, part of the Reformation which swept over Europe in the six-

---

perceived the blend of motives which lay behind its utopianism. Thus his suggestive sentence, "Springing from the traditions of the past, from the deep and wordless sense of the tribe, of the organic community, came a desire to intensify the social bond, to strengthen the cohesion of the folk." Perry Miller, *The New England Mind, The Seventeenth Century* (New York, 1937), 440.

24. Dedham's Covenant itself, together with John Allin's account of the founding of the church, demonstrates the Puritans' deliberate imitation of the primitive Christian communities; see *Records* II, III, and Hans Lietzmann, *The Beginnings of the Christian Church* (trans. B. L. Woolf, London, 1937), especially p. 181. For the equivalent syndrome in medieval peasant utopianism, see F. Graus, "Social Utopias in the Middle Ages," *Past and Present*, no. 38 (Dec., 1967), 3–19.

25. Graus, "Social Utopias," 16–17.

teenth and seventeenth centuries and which in its origins and effects was far more than a mere offshoot of the peasant ethos. This new impulse would color the history of Dedham, and indeed it had brought the townsmen there in the first place.[26] Yet somehow when these creatures of the Reformation came to articulate their ideal of social organization, they not only continued but actually perfected and sanctified the ideal of the peasant past. The two sources, Puritan and peasant, were not identical, but by some inscrutable chemistry they came together in a mixture which was as powerful as it was inseparable.[27]

It may be that the catalyst was the American wilderness, whose frightening presence turned the settlers back upon the old ways engrained in them and their forbears. If this was the case, then Puritanism was somewhat incidental to that intensification of the peasant tradition found in Dedham; Puritanism had brought the townsmen face to face with the wilderness and had provided the rhetoric by which their social reaction to this alarming prospect could be sanctified, but it had not directly urged them to their conservative social ideal. Yet it may be also that within Puritanism itself was a fear of the future which tended to send its advocates to the past for their definition of the holy society.[28]

Whatever the exact nature of the mixture, Dedham was at once a Puritan and a peasant utopia. It partook of the desire for a reformed religion which had seized Europeans in all walks of life and at the same time it embraced half-conscious patterns which had arisen in peasant villages long before the discovery of America. It blended these sources into an ideology strong enough to unite men from diverse parts of England into a

26. See particularly chapter 2.
27. The precise modern term would be "synergetic compound."
28. Professor Darrett B. Rutman of the University of New Hampshire is now preparing an essay on this problem of distinguishing the traditional from the innovative in Puritanism, and weighing their relative influence.

coherent social organism. Ironically, what was most uniquely "American" about the policies of earliest Dedham was the intensity of their utopianism. For here in the New World the settlers could heed almost without restriction whatever mysterious fears urged them to reconstruct in new perfection the ancient patterns of social organization.

2

The Heart of Perfection: The Church

DEDHAM WAS NOT to be a theocracy. By law, the Puritan clergy could not become officers of the civil society here or elsewhere in the colony. In some ways, the local church actually came to occupy a position of isolation. A good many of the lay elders of the congregation would play no role in the leadership of the town, while the town government, though it shared control of the business affairs of the church, had so little to do with religious beliefs that references to the Lord appeared in its records only twice in fifty years.

This superficial isolation did not mean that the church was irrelevant to the life of the new community. Quite the contrary, it was in several ways central to the settlers' experience. In the first place, these Englishmen had not left their homes merely to organize their own township. John Allin, their first minister, spoke for most of them when he wrote that only "the hope of enjoying Christ in his ordinances" could have persuaded the emigrants to "forsake dearest relations, parents, brethren, sisters, Christian friends and acquaintances, overlook the dangers and difficulties of the vast seas, the thought whereof was a terror to many, and . . . go into a wilderness where we could forecast nothing but care and temptation." [1] Even before a church was organized, this overriding concern for the implementation of true Christian faith had been written into the town Covenant, ensuring that the townsmen would be Christians in secular life

1. John Allin, *Defense of the Answer Made unto the Nine Questions or Positions Sent from New England* . . . (London, 1648).

as well as in church. Once the church was formed, the inhabitants of the town would assemble several times each week to
hear sermons or lectures in practical piety, most of them would
become members of the church, and church and town officers
together would keep watch over the moral tone of the community. So, if anything, the church was to be the focus of
that revived Christian spirit which had brought the settlers to
America and was to illumine every aspect of their communal
life.

At the same time, the church was intimately related to the
community of Dedham in that both were organized around the
principles of autonomy, exclusiveness, and unity. The local
church emerged as an autonomous congregation whose membership excluded persons who could not prove they had received
saving grace and in which the members were united by a
covenant of love. Although these features were eventually
expected of all churches by the religious authorities of the
colony, the idea of a self-governing corporation of the saved
was not just imposed from above. Founding their church in
the years when the spiritual leaders of Massachusetts were still
groping their way toward a definition of the true Church, the
Dedham townsmen contributed to the growing insistence on
what came to be called "congregationalism" and "the church
of saints." Their church was organized according to their own
vision of religious perfection, a vision which in this respect
was very like their vision of social perfection. Both town and
church partook of a common utopian form whose sources lay
with yet beneath Puritan Christianity, in the Bible yet also
in the ancient enduring motives of peasant communities.

*   *   *

Founding a church was more difficult than founding a town.
For the town, it had been enough to write down the skeletal
social ordinances of the Covenant, whereupon admissions and

allotments had gone forward, but months of painstaking discussion had to pass before a church covenant could be agreed upon. The basic principles were probably clear from the beginning, since they were largely the principles already written into the town Covenant. But in seeking to establish a true church the townsmen were trying to discover the exact means of salvation, a task whose implications were of the utmost importance. When it came down to the fine points of theology, their only authoritative guide was the Bible, a diffuse, obscure, sometimes contradictory book. It is no wonder that the process took time.

They began late in 1637, with a series of meetings open to "all the inhabitants who affected church communion . . . lovingly to discourse and consult together [on] such questions as might further tend to establish a peaceable and comfortable civil society and prepare for spiritual communion." [2] The townsmen, "being from several parts of England," sought to become "further acquainted with the tempers and gifts of one another." The meetings were held on the fifth day of every week at several houses in rotation. After the man of the house had opened proceedings with a prayer, each person asked questions or talked as he felt the need, all "humbly and with a teachable heart not with any mind of cavilling or contradicting." "Which order," wrote John Allin, "was so well observed as generally all such reasonings were very peaceable, loving and tender, much to edification." The weeks of mutual exploration probably spared them many later contentions.

"After which," Allin noted, "we proceeded to such as more properly concerned the scope of our meetings." Facing the task of gathering a church, those in attendance hammered out thir-

2. This and following quotations concerning the foundation of the church are from John Allin's "Brief History of the Church of Christ . . . at Dedham in New England," written shortly after the events it describes and reprinted in *Records*, II, 1–21. The genesis of the process of founding a church in Puritan New England is discussed in Morgan, *Visible Saints*.

teen questions and answering propositions containing the doctrinal base of the proposed congregation. They began with a
clean slate. Did they, as a collection of Christian strangers in
the wilderness, have any right to assemble with the intention of
establishing a church? The answer was positive. As they understood the meaning of the Bible, "the right to pray, fast, consult,
and institute a church" flowed from the relation of individual
believers to Christ; they did not have to be either members of
or under the supervision of an existing church in order to begin
a new one. Assured of the legality of their endeavor, the par-
ticipants went on to list the canons of the perfect church.

The second proposition set forth the universal "duties of
Christian love," these being "to exhort, admonish, privately
comfort, to communicate and improve any gift . . ., to relieve
the wants of each other." Typically, the rule of love was placed
before the complexities of doctrine. But the third question
forced them to leave behind a simple fellowship of love; it asked
"whether having these privileges of Christian communion [ques-
tion one] and being bound by such duties [of love, question two],
we may not rest in such a condition and look no further?" The
reply was firm: "Negatively, we may not, but [must] seek for a
further union even such as may . . . convey unto us all the
ordinances of Christ's instituted worship, both because it is the
command of God . . . and also because the spiritual condition
of every Christian is such as stand in need of all instituted
ordinances for the repair of the spirit." The Quakers would one
day shrink back from this conclusion, resting content with a
loving fellowship of believers, leaving to each man the details
of his own worship. The Puritans were more skeptical about the
ability of the individual to find a valid form of worship. Putting
their faith instead in the church institutions which the Bible
seemed to demand, they moved beyond.

The essential feature of "Christ's instituted worship" was
spelled out in the answer to the fourth question. The church
fellowship was to be restricted to "visible saints . . . agreeing to

live together in spiritual communion . . . in the use of all the holy instituted ordinances . . . of the gospel." Only congregations of saints could exercise the ordinances of Christian worship, since by the word of Christ only they were pure enough.[3] How then were visible saints to be distinguished from other men? The fifth proposition replied, "a profession of faith and holiness [and] the fruit of it as makes it visible makes a man fit matter for a visible church." God alone knew the identity of the saints, knew who had received grace and who would one day be elected to join the company of the saved. But a person's public behavior and his profession of faith—his spiritual autobiography—could serve to identify him as a visible saint, almost surely one of the elect of God. By measuring candidates' lives and experiences against their own, the members of a church could select those who were "fit matter" to join. The rest, excluded, would attend dutifully the sermons delivered in the meetinghouse, awaiting the spiritual quickening that might come to carry them past the examination and into the inner communion. The sixth proposition provided that the saints thus selected were to sign a covenant which would knit them "firmly in the bond of love . . . and a sweet communion," serving also as a contract with God for the observance of the forms ordained in the Bible.

Yet how could those present examine candidates or write a church covenant if there were among them no proven saints? To ask a neighboring congregation to select the first saints and founding members would be unthinkable, since each congregation was responsible directly to Christ for the purity of its standards. The problem was solved by asking a few likely men to "join by way of confession and profession of faith" to one another in order to assure themselves that they were suitable

3. Communion, the baptism of children, and the election of officers were reserved for the visible saints. Other ordinances of Christian worship (especially preaching) were available to persons who were not members of the church; but all ordinances were, in the strict sense, "exercised" (dispensed) by the congregation of saints.

founders of a church. After testing each other for sainthood, these pillars of the church could then sign a covenant and judge the spiritual qualifications of applicants. "But," it was added, "the number and what persons should first join is not much material, so they be such as are living stones . . . and also be of that innocency of life as may invite others more willingly to join to them."

The remaining six questions and propositions filled in the broad spaces of this framework, listing the ordinances of the church (baptism, communion, marriage, preaching), naming its offices. At the end the faith in "brotherly love" was reaffirmed. Doctrines had been spun out with infinite care and legalistic turns of speech, but before and after all doctrine came the rules of the spirit which were to lead the way to an enduring church.

The search for doctrine having ended, the search for the "living stones" on which to found the church began. In the early Spring of 1638, ten men chosen by all present began to meet separately "after solemn invocations and humiliation . . . before the Lord, . . . to open their conditions and declare the workings of God in their souls . . . [and to] approve or leave out as the Lord should give us to judge of every one's conditions or fitness for the work." The goal was a lengthy mutual testing of the men who had been chosen likely candidates for "soundness of grace." Each was to speak all he knew of himself or the others with neither ambition nor reticence. After "many meetings" six of the ten were found suitable, as was John Hunting, a new arrival in the town, while Edward Alleyn was considered a strong possibility. Of the remaining three, Joseph Kingsbury, still "stiff and unhumbled," and Thomas Morse, "not being able to hold forth anything that might persuade the company of a work of saving grace," agreed to suspend their candidacies for the moment.

The eight most likely submitted themselves to "a meeting or conference of the whole town," asking the inhabitants, "if they had any offences or grievances in their spirits from any of us and knew any just cause which might move us to leave out any, that

now they would faithfully and plainly deal with such a one."
Though there were no bruised feelings in Dedham, several men
from out of town arose to complain of offenses at the hands of
Edward Alleyn. His replies satisfied everyone, so all eight men
gained the unqualified approval of the meeting. John Allin,
Ralph Wheelock, John Luson, John Frary, Eleazer Lusher,
Robert Hinsdell, John Hunting, and Edward Alleyn were the
products of six months of doctrinal debate followed by six
months more of intense mutual examination. A wrong step, the
misreading of the Word or of a man's character, could have
threatened the purity of the church. Now, in November of 1638,
nearly two years after the General Court had created the new
township and a year after the first exploratory meetings of the
settlers, the covenant could be signed and the church instituted.

Preparations for the ceremony went forward in an atmosphere of joyful expectation. Invitations were sent out to the
churches and magistrates of the colony, asking them to send
representatives to see "that nothing might be done therein
against the rule of the gospel." The men of Dedham had every
reason to ask the "advice and counsel of the churches" and
"countenance and encouragement of the magistrates," for they
had been careful in searching out the rule of the gospel. They
did not expect objections. In case the authorities should decide
to object, Dedham reminded them that strict congregational
theory meant that each congregation was responsible only to
Christ, implying that any objections which were not couched as
advice would be looked upon as unwarranted interference. On
the chosen day John Allin read aloud the founders' profession of
faith. He asked that it be criticized "faithfully and plainly." No
criticism was voiced. The covenant, which included a promise
"to live together . . . according to the rule of love in . . . faith-
ful mutual helpfulness in the ways of God for the spiritual and
temporal good and comfort on one another," was likewise approved by all present. The eight pillars signing the document,
the church was begun at that moment.

Not even this ended the process. Though candidates for

regular membership could now be heard and admitted, there were no officers. Without a minister, a teacher, or an elder there could be no preaching and no communion. Still another "tender" search began; after more months of humble discussions another ceremony followed, at which Allin was ordained as minister, John Hunting as elder, and the church was fully constituted.

So the utopian theory behind the foundation of the church proved much the same as that behind the foundation of the town; it is summarized in the words autonomy, exclusiveness, and unity. But the parallel had not been exact. In the case of the town, exclusiveness and unity were complementary virtues; strangers were kept off in order that the inhabitants might live undisturbed under the rule of love. The theory did not work that simply in the case of the church. While religious exclusiveness protected the pure church and fostered a close fellowship among the saints, it was potentially disruptive in the wider context of the town, since some of the inhabitants of the town might not meet the spiritual standard required for membership in the church. What if tension should arise between those inhabitants who were members and those who were not? The drive for perfection in the church could lead to conflict in the town! Recognizing this source of dissonance in their utopian scheme, the townsmen had taken great care to balance the exclusiveness of the church with a larger unity. They had created not only a pure church whose members were closely bound together, but also a church which the whole town had helped to create, could agree to support, would regularly attend, and perhaps could expect one day to enter. Should that day come, church and town, co-existent creations of the same impulse, would become virtually identical, no more than two aspects of one perfect Christian community.

*   *   *

Harmony continued to prevail as the congregation was formed and settled into the life of the town. The inherent ex-

clusiveness of the church was all but forgotten for the first twenty years. Admissions during this period were frequent enough to make the membership of the congregation and the town substantially the same. Seventy percent of the adult men in town in 1648 had become members, as had many of their wives; in other families wives alone were members. Eighty percent of the children born in Dedham between 1644 and 1653 were baptized, the membership of one or both parents qualifying them for the sacrament. Women joined in equal numbers with men. Servants joined their masters in the company of saints, and men of modest means mingled freely in the fellowship with men of substance.[4] When the wife of Robert Hinsdell became "fearful and not able to speak in public, . . . fainting away there," the church refused to let the customary public examination keep out a shy saint; she was admitted on the basis of a private conference. The congregation may have preferred "tender-hearted and hopefull" Christians such as Daniel Fisher or the "tender and brokenhearted" Henry Phillips, but the proud were gathered in as well: "Jonathan Fairbanke, notwithstanding he had long stood off from the church upon some scruples about public profession of faith and the covenant, yet after divers loving conferences . . ., he made such a declaration of his faith and conversion to God and profession of subjection to the ordinances of Christ in this church that he was readily and gladly received by the whole church." Even "stiff" Joseph Kingsbury was not left out; rejected as a founding member in 1638, he entered the fold in 1641. Though nonmembers were consequently rare, the town did not discriminate against them; John Haward and Samuel Morse were elected to public offices before they had joined the

---

4. If in the aggregate the church members were slightly more wealthy than the few nonmembers, this was primarily because the latter tended to be younger persons who had as yet had little time in which to acquire either grace or estate. If there was any discrimination, it was on the basis of age rather than of wealth, and this "discrimination" may have been the result of a voluntary reluctance on the part of young persons to seek membership. See a later discussion in this chapter.

congregation. In view of the high rate of admissions, the townsmen may have assumed that Haward and Morse would be
members soon enough.[5]

Much of the good order of the church was attributable to
John Allin, who had steered the townsmen through the compli-
cations of their search and urged on them the humility which
had eased the way. His account of the process and his public
writings in defense of New England Puritanism reveal that Allin
valued Christian love above theological perfection. It was no
accident that the sermon which his parishoners later chose to
reprint as a memorial was entitled, "The Lord Jesus, His Legacy
of Peace." The sermon stated the theme of Allin's career: ". . .
all troubles and all dangers shall not hurt this peace, but all shall
work together to the furtherance of their everlasting peace,
which . . . will guard your hearts against all evil whatsoever."[6]

While he lived, Dedham's first minister was given material
proof of the respect of the town. His salary of sixty to eighty
pounds yearly was a handsome sum in a society in which a total
estate of 500 pounds meant wealth. On each division of public
land his name was near the top of the list, his share one of the
largest.[7] More important to Allin was the fact that this gener-
osity was entirely voluntary. Not a word about the sordid details
of collections or arrears in salary could be found in the records
during his tenure. Both members and nonmembers gave silently,
freely, as the spirit moved them.

Fifteen years after the founding of the church, Edward
Johnson remarked that the religious community in Dedham had
"continued in much love and unity from their first foundation."

5. *Records,* II, 21ff. lists admissions. The quotations are from
14, 21, 24, 29; *Records,* II, 21ff., III, 69, 77 for the points about Haward
and Morse.

6. *Records,* II, 1–21; Allin, *Defense of the Answer;* Allin, "The
Lord Jesus, His Legacy of Peace" (Cambridge, 1671), also in E. Burgess,
Dedham Pulpit (Boston, Mass., 1840).

7. See *Records,* III, IV; Allin's estate inventory is on file at the
Probate Office of the Suffolk County Courthouse.

The record bore him out. No open disputes had flared within the congregation, no one in the town had criticized the saints. Johnson's observation was included in his *Wonder Working Providence,* a breathless account of the achievements of the Puritans in New England. Considering the religious quarrels which had divided men in England, it is possible to understand why Johnson added Dedham's "love and unity" to his list of the many wonders wrought by God in the northern wilderness.[8]

* * *

Despite the success in establishing harmony, it was ultimately an attachment to exclusiveness which most marked the Dedham church. Throughout the colony the second half of the seventeenth century brought challenges to the doctrine of a church of saints. Most of the men and women of the emigration had been seekers after God with their whole hearts, as their actions testified. The experience of grace had come to them often, if not easily. But what about their children, brought young to America or born there never having known the heresies and persecutions of Anglican England? Would they be so ready to feel the work of divine grace on their sinful souls? If they did not, they could not become members of the church. What would become of their children in turn, for the children of nonmembers could not even be baptized? And what would become of the Puritan Church in the colonies as fewer became members and fewer still were introduced into its traditions by baptism? As the first generation died off, the covenants would lack adherents and the Church would dwindle to a handful of saints. Along with many other communities, Dedham came face to face with this dilemma. From 1653 to 1657 only eight inhabitants were admitted to membership; none joined from 1657 to 1662. The

8. Edward Johnson, *Wonder-Working Providence of Sions Saviour in New England,* edited by J. F. Jameson (New York, 1910), 180. For examples of disputes, see Edmund S. Morgan, *The Puritan Dilemma, The Story of John Winthrop* (Boston, Mass., 1958).

young men and women of the second generation were coming of age but were not joining the church. They were not hostile; they simply failed to undergo the profound emotional conversion required for sainthood. By 1662 nearly half the adult men in town were not members and their numbers were growing steadily as ever more young men grew to maturity. Since their children were not eligible for baptism, the proportion of infants baptized into the church fell from eighty to forty percent.[9] Yet, while the ministers of the colony took steps to head off disaster, the Dedham congregation clung to the church of saints.

The ministers convened a Synod in 1662. Retreating from advocacy of the pure church of saints, they created an additional "half-way" membership bound by a "half-way" covenant of its own.[10] Under the new covenant the children of the saints could become members entitled to all ordinances except communion if they would show that they understood, believed, and would try to obey the word of God as revealed in the Bible. By avoiding the requirement of an inner experience of grace, the new membership opened the churches to the second generation and guaranteed that the third generation would be baptized. John Allin volunteered to defend the new doctrine against its conservative critics, having seen in his own town the pernicious effects of the old way.[11] But, alas for Allin, his own congregation would not compromise its desire for perfection. The members refused to allow "half-way" members to join the saints in the church so that the Dedham church narrowed still further. The disagreement never became a dispute; Allin stayed on to the day of his death, honored if not always heeded. But there could be no doubt that the congregation was determined to preserve the pure church that the members had so carefully constructed.

9. *Records,* I, *Births, Marriages and Deaths;* II, 21ff.; and tax lists in IV.

10. See Perry Miller, "The Half-Way Covenant," *New England Quarterly,* VI (1933) 676–715, and Morgan, *Visible Saints.*

11. John Allin, *Animadversions on the Antisynodalia Americana* (Cambridge, Mass., 1664).

Other reluctant congregations abandoned resistance in 1671, when an overwhelming majority of the towns' representatives to the General Court voted support of the doctrinal authority of the clergy, but Daniel and Joshua Fisher, representatives from Dedham, dissented.[12]

Though it never brought either the congregation or the town to open argument, the path of resistance was a hard one. A temporary reverse followed Allin's death late in 1671. Remorse and repeated refusals from ministers offered the vacant pulpit persuaded the congregation to back down. The change of heart was sincere: "We acknowledge the fault to be ours, not that of our pastor, who brought us up properly and showed the way and the word clearly and long . . . [especially the] church duty to the children of the covenant born of us and growing up with us as members of the church by divine instruction and so the proper subjects of . . . church privileges . . . . We are now under the conviction of our total neglect of the practice of this doctrine . . . . We do therefore hereby solemnly and in the fear of God . . . acknowledge all such children of the covenant . . . to be joint members of this particular visible church together with ourselves . . . . We apply and cry earnestly unto God for his spirit and grace whereby we may be all enabled to stand fast in one spirit with one mind striving together not only in faith but the order of the gospel that both may abide with us from generation to generation forever." [13]

But the issue did not rest there. From 1685 to 1692 the church was once more without a minister. Once again likely young Harvard men were offered the pulpit and once gain they refused. Late in 1691 the congregation at last put an end to all resistance: "The church of Christ in full communion . . . do

12. Massachusetts Historical Society manuscript in *Photostats* file, June, 1671; *The Records of the Governor and Company of Massachusetts Bay* . . . , IV, part 2, 492.

13. Massachusetts Historical Society Manuscripts, in the catalogue under "Dedham, 1672."

now by their vote declare . . . that the declaration of the synod
[of 1662] and the doctrine of their late reverend pastor is according to the mind of Christ and do resolve through his help and
grace to practice accordingly." [14] A minister was soon found
and the issue never arose again.

Such enduring exclusiveness is a formidable mark of the
intensity with which the men of Dedham sought perfection in
their religion. The attachment to a pure church was not easily
loosened by time and circumstance; fathers passed on to their
sons the adherence to the old principle of membership, and the
sons who did not become saints did not object to the narrowness
of the church. Originally justified by Puritan ideology, the com-
mitment to exclusiveness gained its persistence from what has
been called "tribalism," the eternal desire to protect the ways of
the community against the encroachment of change.[15] Like the
town, the church sprang from a thirst for perfection whose
origins were deep and whose complex effects permeated every
part of the common existence.

14. Manuscripts in the vault of the Dedham Historical Society.
15. "Tribalism" was first applied to the Puritans by Edmund S.
Morgan, *The Puritan Family* (1944; Rev. Ed., New York, 1966), ch. 7.
For an example of the use of religious organization (and ceremony)
to re-enforce peasant communal corporatism in a Catholic country, see
"Religious Aspects of the Social Organization of a Castilian Village,"
Susan Tax Freeman, 1969, *American Anthropologist*.

3

The Pattern of Communal Politics

"AT A GENERAL TOWN MEETING it was voted as followeth," "It is by general consent ordered," "Ordered by general consent"—the expressions of what today is called town meeting democracy were current in this seventeenth-century village. Yet it is not correct to say that the myth of the democratic New England town has a firm basis in fact reaching back to the beginnings of this town. Even to raise the question is to do an injustice to the past. Between the seventeenth century and the twentieth a conceptual revolution took place, a revolution in which the banners of popular democracy raised high by the nineteenth century were victorious. Land of the free, Andy Jackson, the people's President, I'm as good as the next man, Tippecanoe and Tyler too, torchlight parades and barbecues—the men of early Dedham knew none of these; the present age cannot escape them. From the time of the democratic revolution all politics has been the politics of universal manhood suffrage and correspondingly of "deals" for the common man whether New or Fair or Square. Questions about the political style of the distant past tend to be colored by this subsequent layer of experience. Inquiries are prejudiced by the knowledge that a tradition of popular democracy has become America's gift to the world. Actually the very term "democracy" was rarely used in the seventeenth century and was then devoid of the favorable overtones now attached to it. It is anachronistic, therefore pointless, to look for anything resembling modern democracy in early Dedham.

What was the style of political life in this long-ago utopia? It was a thing unto itself, full of contradictions which the modern mind is hard put to resolve but which were no contradictions at all to the mind of the seventeenth century.[1]

* * *

The town meeting was the original and protean vessel of local authority. The founders of Dedham had met to discuss the policies of their new community even before the General Court had defined the nature of town government. Acting in March, 1635, the Court gave a broad mandate to all such assemblies of townsmen; they were authorized to make bylaws not repugnant to the laws of the colony and to "choose their own particular officers." [2] Shortly after receiving this official sanction the Dedham meeting called into being its companion in local government, the board of selectmen. On May 3, 1639, the town resolved, "whereas it has been found by long experience that the general meeting of so many men in one [assembly to consider] of the common affairs thereof has wasted much time to no small damage, and business is nothing furthered thereby, it is therefore now agreed by general consent that these seven men hereunder named we do make choice of and give them full power to contrive, execute, and perform all the business and affairs of this our whole town—unto the first of the tenth month next." Yearly thereafter the meeting chose seven men to act as a town executive with "full power" over most affairs.[3] Because

1. The discussions of politics in this and in the seventh chapter are expanded in "The Evolution of Massachusetts Town Government, 1640 to 1740," by Kenneth A. Lockridge and Alan Kreider, *William and Mary Quarterly,* XXIII, (1966), 549–74.

2. *Records,* III, 1–2; *Records of the Governor and Company of Massachusetts Bay* . . . , I, 172.

3. *Records,* III, 53. The General Court recognized the innovation, which was soon employed by nearly all towns, in the Body of Liberties of 1641; William H. Whitmore, ed., *A Bibliographical Sketch of the Laws of the Massachusetts Colony from 1630 to 1686* (Boston, Mass.,

political power in the town (as in most towns) soon polarized around the meeting and around these "select-men," the story of communal politics must be woven around these institutions.

John Gay wanted to build a barn nearer his fields. The trouble was, the best site for a barn was on public land. At the end of February 1667 he went to a meeting of the board of selectmen and asked for "an enlargement of land near his land beyond Andrew Duane's for the setting of a barn." The board sent Daniel Fisher, a selectman since 1650 who eventually occupied the office thirty-two times together with the novice Thomas Fuller, to "view the place desired and make return of what they judge meet in the case." Since he had already taken up his share of the recent divisions of town land, Gay did not have any land coming to him. Instead, Fisher and Fuller worked out a swap; Gay would give the town the right to run a road across his house lot in the village in return for the two acres of town land he had selected as the site for the barn. Four acres of swamp leading from Gay's fields down to the Charles River would be thrown in to overcome his reluctance at the prospect of cart traffic rumbling beneath his windows. It was not a bad bargain. Anyway the only recourse would be an appeal to the next meeting of the whole town and the approach of planting season made that delay unwise. Gay accepted. The selectmen approved, sealing the bargain two weeks after the request.[4]

Much of the power of the Dedham selectmen derived from a thousand variations on the theme of John Gay's barn. Thomas Aldridge's widowed mother wanted to take up her proprietary share of the "Natick Dividend" near her house rather than out by Natick as was expected of everyone else. Michael Metcalf said that his grandfather had forgotten to claim a rightful share

---

1890), 49. See also *Records of the Governor and Company of Massachusetts Bay in New England,* II, 4, 6–9, 163, 180. Unlike the selectmen, the town's lesser officers did not have broad discretionary powers, being confined to one or two highly specific functions.

4. *Records,* IV, 147–48, 154.

in a former division; the records should be checked, the right recognized, and the land granted. Joseph Kingsbury had been assigned some "very bad land" and sought to trade it for better land elsewhere. Francis Chickering needed a little triangle of common land so that he could straighten the fence around his field.[5] They came to the selectmen, Gay, Aldridge, Metcalf, Kingsbury, Chickering, all the members of this agricultural town who wanted something from the public domain.

Indeed, the selectmen enjoyed almost complete control over every aspect of local administration. They determined the guilt or innocence of men accused of breaking the bylaws. Who was responsible, the farmer whose ill-kept cattle had escaped to trample someone else's grain or the fellow whose tumbledown fences had let the straying beasts into the fields? The selectmen would decide. Questions of the location of highways and of men's ways of access to their fields came up frequently. These entailed touchy issues of property rights—the rights of the public versus the individual or of one landowner versus another—customarily resolved by the selectmen. Townsmen who took firewood or hay from the common lands would risk a fine unless they had the prior approval of the selectmen. The seven men acted as the guardians of the social order by investigating rumors of disorderly conduct and dictating stern remedies. It was a rare townsman who did not find himself either wanting or having to attend the selectmen at several of their meetings each year,[6] and it was a rare selectman who did not find himself judging most of his fellow townsmen in the course of a year. The full board met in formal session about ten times yearly, more often in less formal groups of four or five. The business brought before them might take a few minutes and a few lines in the town book, but it could as easily take much of the day and several pages in the record. The typical panel

5. *Records,* III, 201; IV, 71, 148, 153–54.
6. *Records,* III, IV, V, abound in examples. Henceforth, pages will be cited only where examples are singular or scarce.

of selectmen had accumulated a vast store of experience in the intricacies of town life, had dispensed favors, punished wrong-doers, heard and settled problems by the score. As in the politics of any age, power led to experience and experience enhanced power.

Not merely in the trivia of administration but in every major sphere of political activity the selectmen developed a strong initiative. Appointive powers were shared with the meeting, the selectmen naming fenceviewers, sealers of weights and measures, and others of the lesser functionaries. When presented with a difficult problem, the board would appoint a special committee of townsmen instructed to investigate and report back. The power of the purse fell largely to the selectmen, who estimated the needs of the town and periodically levied taxes. This was an especially sensitive task, for it involved determining how much each townsman was obliged to pay. The town's chief legislators, the selectmen promulgated important bylaws without prior consultation with or subsequent approval by the general meeting. These ranged from the usual laws concerning livestock and fences to a broad statute imposing controls on whatever mines might be discovered, enacted in 1647.[7]

The initiative of the board reached a peak in its control over the functioning of the town meeting itself. Colony law required one or two annual gatherings for electoral purposes, but beyond this the selectmen called whatever general meetings seemed necessary. They called very few. When they did, they prepared a detailed agenda to guide the meeting. The agenda included proposals for action, and it was not unusual for the procedure to run as follows: "an order being presented already drawn by the selectmen—being put to vote it was voted in the affirmative, confirming the same for a town order." [8]

7. *Records,* III, 84, 119; V, 50–51, 143, 168, 173, will give examples of points not immediately obvious from a look at any part of the records.

8. See *Records,* IV, 35, 74–75, 123, 222; the quotation is from

The line between such strong leadership and complete domination might have been crossed with a little effort. In some English parishes (the English original of the town) the select vestrymen had begun with legal powers comparable to those of the Dedham selectmen and had evolved past the stage of strong leadership into uncontrollable, self-perpetuating oligarchies.[9] Not the least of the circumstances which kept this from happening in Dedham was the care with which the board of selectmen exercised its manifold powers. Every request was duly heard, duly investigated. The plea of a selectman received the same treatment as the plea of any townsman. Votes of the town were executed without hesitation, and not one incumbent questioned the town's right to elect another man in his place.

Who were the selectmen? As selectmen they were the most powerful men in town. As men, they were few in number, old, relatively rich, and saints of the church.

Forty-three men served as selectmen between 1639 and 1687, averaging eight terms each. This persistent returning of men to the office reflects the town's inclination to leave a man in office if he passed the test of his first few terms. The inclination went so far in some cases that the town was in fact led by a very few men: ten men, perhaps five percent of the adult males living in Dedham before 1687, were returned to office so often that they filled sixty percent of the selectmen's posts, thereby supplying sixty percent of the local leadership. The ten averaged twenty terms apiece in careers ranging from fourteen to thirty-two terms, careers which they like most selectmen began in middle life, usually about age forty. In the seventeenth century a man of forty could hardly expect to live past seventy, so, once

---

IV, 125. As will be seen in chapter 7, the power of the selectmen was to undergo a radical change in the post-1686 period, as indeed was the whole political style of the town. The style depicted here was unique to the seventeenth-century town.

9. Sidney and Beatrice Webb, *English Local Government . . . ,* I, *The Parish and the County* (New York, 1906), 39, 41n., 42–43, 173ff.

embarked on their careers, these ten men served for most of their remaining lives. The duty was not continuous—every experienced selectman taking an occasional year off—but it was almost continuous. And even when out of office each of the ten was asked to lend advice or lead emergency committees. Another fifteen men occupied the office for four to twelve terms, averaging ten. They supplied another thirty percent of the leadership. The careers of the men in this group tended to be cut short by premature death or by departure from the town. A last group of eighteen men served one to three terms, less than two on the average, and accounted for only ten percent of the leadership.[10] By and large these were the rejects of a system which sought strong leaders and having found one returned him to power as often and as long as he was available.

The selectmen were comparatively wealthy men, both because they had lived long enough to wring prosperity from the stubborn soil and because the voters liked to elect the more substantial of the mature townsmen. The typical selectman's estate placed him somewhere in the richest quarter of the townsmen. The less well off were not called as often as their more prosperous fellow townsmen, nor were they called back as often. Twelve of the twenty-seven most wealthy men on the 1666 tax list acted as selectman for a total of 100 terms, while of the sixty-three less wealthy taxpayers only seven served for a mere forty-one terms. Wealth was not everything—some men from the lower ranks were called to office—but it helped. How much it helped can be seen from the cases of the ten leading

10. Averages are rounded off. There were minor exceptions to the rule of seven men a year. The information is from *Records* I, III, IV, V (records of births and deaths, and of yearly elections, etc.). Judgments of the data are, again, based on an implicit comparison with the post-1686 period, discussed in chapter 7. Demographic information is treated more fully in chapter 4. The ten were Eleazer Lusher (first elected 1639), John Dwight (1639), Francis Chickering (1641), Peter Woodward (1643), Timothy Dwight (1644), Joshua Fisher (1649), Daniel Fisher (1650), John Hunting (1658), Daniel Pond (1661), and Thomas Fuller (1661).

selectmen. By the time they reached their third terms (the point at which the long-term leaders tended to be kept on and the others set aside) all ten were in the upper third, seven were in the upper sixth, and five were in the top tenth of the taxpayers.[11]

The predominance of men of substance is all the more remarkable in a society whose spectrum of wealth was not in actual fact very wide. From its beginnings and for some time thereafter, the town contained neither a distinct class of English-style gentry nor seventeenth-century versions of the millionaire. The voters had to create their own "aristocrats" by picking relatively wealthy farmers and keeping them in positions of leadership, which they did. In this practice they echoed the decision of the founders to reward with extra land such relative "rank and quality" as a few of the first settlers had managed to acquire in England. Both actions stemmed from the same desire to balance with a measure of hierarchy and respect, the collectivism of the covenantial ideology and the tendency toward middle-class homogeneity resulting from the nature of the exodus and from the primitive economy.[12]

11. Tax lists in *Records*, III, IV, V. All lists and all selectmen at all stages during and preceding their careers have been considered. The 1666 list is in *Records,* IV, 119ff., and is not an extreme example. Regarding the top ten selectmen, see *Records,* III, 152–53, 213–14; IV, 37–38, 90–91, 104–05. In three cases the evidence is of necessity drawn from a time later than the third term, but still early in the man's career. See chapter 4 for a description of the social structure.

12. See chapter 4 for a discussion of the relatively limited spread of the hierarchy of wealth, which in fact emerged among the middle class immigrants who settled Dedham.

The political practice of "creating aristocrats" did not arise simply because the more wealthy men alone could devote the necessary time to public duties and therefore *had* to be preferred over men struggling to make a living. In neighboring Watertown—which had a comparable social and political structure in all other respects—the voters ranged widely and evenly through the levels of taxpayers in selecting leaders (see Lockridge and Kreider, "The Evolution of Massachusetts Town Government"). Dedham's voters could have done the same, but chose instead to elevate the more wealthy of their fellows. No doubt the voters saw the advan-

A large majority of the selectmen were members of the church, a circumstance which added to their prestige and which strengthened the bonds between the town corporation and the church corporation but did not necessarily reflect a local preference for saints. It happened that the selectmen with the longest careers—nine of the leading ten for example—had established themselves at a time when most men were church members. They continued to serve in the following decades, occupying places that might otherwise have been given to younger men maturing in the years when church membership was no longer so characteristic.

The influence of the most prominent selectmen went considerably beyond the limits of excutive functions within the town. It was these men whom the town sent as its representatives to the one superior it recognized, the General Court of the colony. All but five of the years to 1685 saw one of the ten sitting as Dedham's man in Boston and three of them—Eleazer Lusher, Daniel Fisher, and Joshua Fisher—virtually monopolized the post after 1650. Lusher achieved distinction in colonial circles by his election as Assistant, a rank surpassed only by the Governor and Deputy Governor. During the ten years he held the honor (1663-1673) Lusher was a one-man ministry of all talents, acting now as diplomat, now as judge, now as mediator in the convolutions of high Puritan politics. Daniel Fisher rose to become Speaker of the House of Deputies in 1680 and after three years in that powerful role he moved up to the rank of Assistant, dying not long after. These were men of many distinctions, rich in knowledge of a world otherwise little known in Dedham. They bridged the gap between the ethnocentric utopia in the woods and the larger spheres of English history,

---

tages in time and dedication that would accrue from the selection of more wealthy men, but the case of Watertown shows that there were no economic or political forces that *required* men to elect the wealthy for these reasons alone. Obviously, the Dedham voters' political ideology also involved innate respect for, rather than suspicion of, the wealthy.

whose operations were even then moving toward a day in which such backwoods utopias could no longer exist. For the time being, they were able to protect their community while doing its tasks in the outside world.[13]

The men who occupied the town's most powerful office were men of immense prestige, but there was another side to their character. As mentioned, their restraint in office was consistent, and in or out of office there is no indication that they treated one another to special favors. They worked hard, giving their time without salary or so much as an honorary title to ease the burden. During some busy months a third of their time would not be their own. Their relative wealth was the town's profit, since their incomes were enought to free the leaders from the worst distractions of a struggle for subsistence. All had been apprentices in the art of government, each having spent several years in the grubby lower echelons of local service. Beginning perhaps as fenceviewer or (alas) hogreeve, each submitted himself to the town's watchful eye. Each had avoided giving offense yet earned the necessary respect as he moved up toward the highest office. Most important, each selectman had been *chosen* by his neighbors. The town wanted these men, called them back repeatedly, elected them to other high posts and to the leadership of its militia company. If the town was an oligarchy, it was a peculiar oligarchy.

*   *   *

The repeated fact that the selectmen were, after all, elected, naturally brings attention back to the town meeting. Surely here was the touchstone of local politics. But it was an elusive touchstone, if indeed there was such a thing in the complex patterns of Dedham's political life.

13. *Records,* IV, Appendix, lists the terms and illustrates the activities of the representatives. See also the card catalog, Massachusetts archives, Basement, State House, Boston, under "Lusher" and "Fisher."

In theory, the power of the town meeting knew no limit. The town had called the board of selectmen into existence and could as easily abolish the institution altogether. On occasion the town would reaffirm the broad mandate of power given to the board and in the very fact of affirmation confirm the ultimate power of the meeting. In a memorable upset in 1660 the town actually went so far as to negative the proposal, "whether they [the selectmen] should have the same power their predecessors have had" and underlined their dissatisfaction by voting out of office every single incumbent—though the pique soon passed. Theoretical power might be translated in very specific ways into real power any time the townsmen assembled. They might pass bylaws, appoint special committees of their own, or grant small favors to petitioners; they customarily admitted new townsmen and appointed many lower officers. Anything the selectmen could do, they could do. Just to make sure the selectmen did their job well, the meeting would sometimes bring up for approval all the acts and accounts of their executive.[14] The yearly elections gave the town a fine tool for use against its leaders, for not only could an entire board be removed but also any one selectman could be singled out for vengeance and left in limbo for one year, two, three, or forever.

The voting membership of the meeting was generally wide enough to include a fair majority of the townsmen, so most men had a voice in local affairs and most could vote to remove an errant selectman. Though the colony law concerning local suffrage shifted with the changing attitudes of the colonial authorities toward the franchise, and though the consistency of the law's application in the town is questionable, some generalizations are safe. Up to seventy percent of the male taxpayers were eligible under a law in effect to 1647, whose chief requirement was church membership. Whatever the law's requirements, the town meetings of the first few years were informal gatherings in

14. *Records*, III, 62, 126, 147; IV, 29. Other meetings are described every few pages in *Records*, III, IV, V.

which all men probably voted. As Dedham interpreted a new law of 1647, only men under twenty-four were ineligible to participate, so the legal suffrage rose to over ninety percent of adult males. An additional requirement of twenty pounds taxable estate imposed in 1658 did little to reduce this; a town voting list for 1666 includes the names of eighty-three of the ninety-one male taxpayers. A law of 1670 raised the amount needed to qualify to a stiff eighty pounds, but took effect slowly since it allowed all town voters who had previously qualified under the old law to continue in the privilege regardless of their estates.[15]

Yet broad as its powers and membership were, the town meeting was essentially passive. It lacked initiative, its veto was quiescent, and its theoretical powers were for the most part symbolic. Meeting on the average only twice a year, the town never had a chance to acquire or apply the consistent expertise of the selectmen. Most meetings stayed close to the agenda prepared by the selectmen and were brief in comparison with those of the board. Formal review of the acts and accounts of the executive was sporadic and at best perfunctory. The townsmen seemed glad to leave most decisions to their leaders, often "referring to the selectmen" to "prepare and ripen the answer." Whatever the answer, it would not be challenged; the town never presumed to replace a substantive decision of the selectmen with its own will. The upset of 1660 was the single occasion on which the town used its theoretical right to withdraw the power of the selectmen and the only time the annual election was used to remove an entire panel of seven men.[16] Year after year for half

15. The most readily accessible summary of the suffrage laws is in B. Katherine Brown "Freemanship in Puritan Massachusetts," *American Historical Review,* LIX (1954), 865–83. Some of Mrs. Brown's interpretations should not be considered final. See *Records,* II, 13–39; III, 20–62, 152, regarding the suffrage to 1647. The list of voters in *Records,* III, 190, confirms the breadth of the 1647–1658 suffrage. For 1666, see *Records,* IV, 119–20, 124. The tax lists in *Records,* IV, V, yield post-1670 figures.

16. See Lockridge and Kreider, "The Evolution of Massachusetts

a century the town elected a wealthy and experienced group of respected friends, took their suggestions, obeyed their bylaws, and left them to run the town without interference.

Furthermore, the law of the colony imposed an increasing degree of narrowness on the right to political participation. Even the comparatively generous local suffrage law of 1647 had excluded young men under twenty-four. The law of 1670 was designed to shut out almost all young men coming of age thereafter. A man might easily be forty before he acquired the necessary eighty pounds of taxable estate or he might never acquire that much. By 1686 only a quarter of the male taxpayers could meet the eighty pound minimum, and though some of the rest could vote because they had been voters before the law of 1670 took effect, nearly half of the taxpayers were not eligible to cast a vote in the town meeting. On the level of the provincial suffrage, the colony law continued to insist that full church members alone were eligible to vote for representatives and Assistants, and church membership in Dedham had fallen to half of the male taxpayers by 1662 and continued to fall thereafter.[17] All in all, if the town was a democracy, it was a most peculiar democracy.

* * *

The system's prime virtue was that it worked. The very ambivalences of the allotment and use of power produced a marvelously stable politics. No man, group of men, or single institution could run away with the town and generally none wanted to try. Supported at every turn by the policy of mediation introduced by the Covenant, this political system gave Dedham fifty years of tranquil government. But to call the

---

Town Government." As with the selectmen's behavior, that of the meeting was to change. For 1660 see *Records,* IV, 29–30.

17. *Records,* II, 13–39; V, tax lists for 1680's. A law of 1664 admitted a few very wealthy non-saints to the colony suffrage; B. K. Brown, "Freemanship in Puritan Massachusetts" discusses but somewhat misunderstands this law.

system successful is still not to describe it: "A successful thing unto itself" is hardly satisfactory. What label fits an oligarchy which was not an oligarchy and a democracy which was no democracy? An excursion into the theory of politics in seventeenth-century Massachusetts offers a tentative answer.

Though a new age of revolutionary political theories was even then beginning, order was still the highest political value in the seventeenth century, as it had been for some centuries before. Thomas Hobbes was no innovator when he observed that human society is naturally inclined to chaos. Hobbes' argument in favor of strong rulers merely secularized the old Christian justification of government. God had given man the capacity to sin, Adam and Eve had sinned, thenceforth men were forever imperfect, forever condemned to fall into immorality and discord. As sin was divinely ordained, so was government. The state existed to restrain the sinful impulse and punish the sinner, not simply because sin was wrong, but because the visible church needed an orderly world in which to fulfill its part of God's plan. A society in which violence interrupted the work of the clergy and unbridled license smothered all examples of virtue was not a proper arena for man's struggle for salvation. The much-maligned James I was only invoking the commonplace when he spoke of the divine right of kings, for traditional theory gave divine sanction to the rulers of the state. Likewise Shakespeare's frequent sallies in praise of order were no more than resounding summations of the deep-rooted spirit of his age. And similarly, much of the "reform" thought of the radical English Protestants of the seventeenth century envisioned not a new and mobile society stressing individual opportunity but rather a social commonwealth whose prime features were security and Christian love.

The Puritans of New England had ample reason to hold to and indeed to extend the seventeenth century's faith in order. Their conception of a whole society bound to God by a covenant made the existence of sin an immediate danger, for to allow sin was to breach the contract with God, thereby inviting his wrath down upon them all. Further, their desire to build a perfect visible church accented the need for a state which would give the church an orderly social setting for its work. Circumstance lent practical force to these arguments; England might use any sign of discord in Massachusetts as an excuse to revoke their charter and take over the government in the name of good order. Such a move would shatter the emigrants' covenant and with it their "city on a hill."

But it does not require Hobbesean skepticism, original sin, or Puritan perfectionism to explain the love of order. All were present, but beneath all, as ever, lay the peasant's inbred fear of chaos. Robbery, extortion, war with its legalized murder—few peasant villages had not lived precariously close to these disasters. Only late in the fifteenth century had the Tudor state ended the bloody baronial feuds which had kept England in turmoil for generations, and it would be at least another century before the age of inchoate popular uprisings would come to an end. The confidence generated by uniform legal order imposed by a central monarchy was new to Englishmen's experience. A little below the surface were folk memories of violence and a longing for peace and certainty.

Such was the background of Dedham's peculiar political behavior. A product of its time, the town Covenant had obliged men to pledge obedience and had gone to some lengths to provide mechanisms for the preservation of order. Men of their time, and also men aware of the dangers involved in founding a perfect society in the wilderness, the townsmen of Dedham took the Covenant to heart. They settled their disputes peacefully and used their electoral powers to elevate a handful of substantial men, leaving in their hands the direction of the community. Sanctified by their election, the leaders of Dedham were further sanctified by their success in keeping order, and thereby they gained re-election repeatedly. Today's praise for democracy as the key to opportunity and for dissent as the harbinger of change would have been grotesquely out of place in such a society, where order outranked opportunity and the changes brought by dissent were not expected to be fruitful.

But a narrow-minded passion for order was not the only source of the town's political behavior. Had it been, there would have been no need for a town meeting. The founders or the colony's Governor could have imposed a set of lifetime rulers who would name their own successors, a complete oligarchy in short. The Puritans' desire for order was more sophisticated than this. Their intense Christianity led them to see in unity rather than in repression the essence of true order. They "demanded that in society all men, at least all regenerate men, be marshalled in one united array . . . . The theorists of New England thought of society as a unity, bound together by inviolable ties; they thought of it not as an aggregation of individuals, but as an organism, functioning for a definite purpose, with . . . all members contributing a definite share . . . ." [18] Therefore, a degree of popular participation was valued, for it would both symbolize and strengthen the unity of all men in the common Christian society. Consent would strengthen unity and that unity would lead to a higher form of order.

So there was in the Puritan political philosophy a door through which the generality could enter to participate in the workings of government. But, at least on the level of the colony's theoreticians and leaders, it was seen as a very narrow door. It was only the saints who could hope to achieve genuine Christian unity, and therefore it was their participation that was the center of concern. Even in their case, "the commanders were not to trim their policies by the desires of the people . . . the officers were above the common men . . . ." The emphasis was on obedience: "When the Lord sets himself over a people,

18. Miller and Johnson, eds., *The Puritans*, I, 182–83; see also Perry Miller, *Orthodoxy in Massachusetts* (Cambridge, Mass., 1933).

he frames them unto a willing and voluntary submission unto him . . . they follow Him not forcedly, but as far as they are sanctified by his grace, they submit willingly to his regiment." The chief participatory acts envisioned were the consent to covenants and the election of a few leaders, acts which would enhance the unity of the participating saints and at the same time give extra cachet to the leaders and to the political frame-work which they had established. Beyond this, participation was likely to be viewed as interference, conducive to disorder.

John Winthrop expressed it in this way: "It is yourselves who have called us to . . . office, and being called by you, we have authority from God." As for liberty, "[the] liberty you are to stand for is a liberty to [do] that only which is good, just, and honest . . . . This liberty is maintained and exercised in a way of subjection to authority." A good subject was to resemble a good wife, for, "the woman's own choice makes such a man her husband; yet being so chosen, he is her lord, and she is to be subject to him, yet in a way of liberty, not of bondage; and a true wife accounts her subjection her honor and freedom . . . ." [19] Though Winthrop's statement exaggerated its authoritarian aspects, the fundamentals of the theory prevailed as the usual ideological justification for popular participation. The colony law continued to insist that church members alone were qualified to vote for colony officers because they alone could be trusted to perceive "that which is good, just, and honest" and to submit themselves to leaders with a like perception.

Perhaps because it was grafted onto a tradition of local consensus and cooperation which had long characterized English peasant communities, the theory had more positive overtones on the local level. The vote was not confined to church members (after 1647) and voters had the right to join in

19. Miller and Johnson, eds., *The Puritans,* I, 183, 190 (from sermons by John Davenport and Peter Bulkely), 206–07 (a speech by Winthrop to the General Court in 1645).

substantive decisions as well as to elect leaders. Still, the town's behavior reveals that the popular voice in Dedham acted in a manner consonant with the Puritan theory of popular participation. Men had signed the Covenant voluntarily and they voluntarily lived according to its commands. Their votes were customarily "by general agreement"—a voluntary consensus. In electing a man, they were asking him to lead a society united in love under the rule of the gospel; in obeying his decisions they were marching together freely in the practice of the "one truth" desired by all. The matching restraint of the selectmen derived more from their own stake in the common unity than from any fear of retaliation. And out of the unity thereby voluntarily achieved, the townsmen also enjoyed an enduring order such as no amount of force could have imposed.

Sixty-nine men of Dedham explicitly approved the prevailing theory in a petition of support sent to the General Court in 1665 to aid the government in its battle against English interference in the affairs of the colony. None of them was qualified to vote in colony elections and some could not participate in the town meeting, yet every last one expressed appreciation of "the great blessing we enjoy . . . in a Godly, righteous, and peaceable government." [20] These men said quite frankly that they valued a government "Godly, righteous, and peaceable" over the limited blessing of the suffrage. In an age in which the suffrage was viewed as one more way of maintaining unity and preserving order, the democrat's worship of the vote was far in the future.

To put it another way, conditions were not ripe for a philosophy of individualism. "The basic sociological findings . . . show that modern individualism depends appreciably upon extensive division of labor, institutional differentiation and cultural diversity." [21] The democracy of differing religions, immigration, urbanization, and contending economic interests was out of the question in the simple society of seventeenth-century

20. *Records,* IV, 276–78.
21. T. Scott Miyakawa, *Protestants and Pioneers, Individualism and Conformity on the American Frontier* (Chicago, Ill., 1964), 233.

Dedham. Diversity had not yet been forced upon men. Until it was, a man's concern would be more with harmonizing himself with the one true way than with protecting his right to vote in a pluralistic world where individual rights had become the only refuge.

The political phenomenon at hand, which might be labeled "Conservative Corporate Voluntarism," actually lies not one but two layers deep in American history. A long distance from the popular democracy of the nineteenth century, it was only beginning to merge into the mechanistic political philosophy which was to characterize eighteenth-century Americans—particularly those eighteenth-century Americans familiar with Enlightenment thought and with contemporary English political theorists.[22] Dedham's political system was intricate, yet ultimately what had made political harmony in Dedham was not a clockwork balance of one power against another but voluntary restraint on the part of all concerned. Eighteenth-century thinkers would de-emphasize the notion of an organic society held together by voluntary restraint. In its place would come an emphasis on the balance of political elements, monarchy, aristocracy, and democracy, each with its own virtues and vices. Ideally, each would contribute its virtues while holding in check the vices of the others. Democracy would contribute the representation of a certain class of interests and the innate good sense of the commonry. The instability of democracy would be cancelled partially by restricting the suffrage to propertied men, partially by the stability of the monarchical and aristocratic elements. The theory of the eighteenth century allowed popular participation at once a greater and a lesser role than its predecessor. By justifying the participation of the commonry in a legislative role and by freeing the suffrage of religious restrictions, it opened a door to the later deification of democracy. Yet by destroying the Puritan notion of popular participation as a holy recognition of the organic unity of men (or at least

22. See Zoltan Haraszti, *John Adams and the Prophets of Progress* (Cambridge, Mass., 1952).

of all believers) in their society, the eighteenth-century outlook stripped the popular voice of a mystical level of human significance which it has since regained, alas, largely in the perverted world of plebescitary totalitarianism.

"Conservative Corporate Voluntarism" in politics, like the closed corporate community in which it operated, was "American" chiefly in that it was a uniquely intense expression of Old World ideals.[23] Only in the most tenuous sense can the roots of modern American democracy be traced back to the political experience of seventeenth-century Dedham. Its limitations and conservative theoretical context notwithstanding, the suffrage *was* significantly wider in Dedham than in England. Both in Dedham and in Massachusetts at large the many officers subject to election by this wider electorate exercised powers which were in the aggregate greater than the powers exercised by elected officers in England. In such innovations lay the deepest foundation of an American participatory mentality, a mentality born of a widened public role in government, which eventually would lead increasing numbers of men to demand a still wider role in their own governance. In this context perhaps the brief political upset in the town of Dedham in 1660 might be seen as the first faint movement of an awakening giant. And perhaps it is possible to see in the divine sanction with which all New England Puritans endowed a limited popular voice the beginnings of the later secular sanctification of Everyman's right to participate which paved the way for the triumph of democracy as a supreme virtue. But it must not be forgotten that modern democracy whether in practice or in theory was a long way in the future. It took far more than moderately wide participation, occasional popular protests, or veiled scriptural justifications to create that democracy.

23. For examples of the relationship of Protestant political theory to government in the Old World, see E. William Monter, *Calvin's Geneva* (New York, 1965); and also Gerald Strauss, "Protestant Dogma and City Government: The Case of Nuremberg," *Past and Present,* No. 36, 38–58.

4

The Pattern of Communal Society

IT HAS BECOME FASHIONABLE to view the settlers of Massachusetts Bay as men more pulled to America by the opportunity to found a new society than pushed there by the persecutions of Anglican England. Michael Metcalf, one of the founders of Dedham and for a time its schoolmaster, would have disagreed violently. On abandoning his homeland and his career as a master weaver in provincial Norwich, Metcalf had written a long letter "to all true professors of Christ's gospel" within that city.[1] Trying to justify his sudden departure from the Puritan community, he spoke of "the great trouble I sustained in the Arch-Deacon's and Bishop's court at the hands of my enemies concerning the matter of bowing as well as for other matters of like consequence." When hauled before the ecclesiastical court he had expertly quoted against the judges their own theologians and the Bible itself, but to his disgust "their learned and invincible arguments to refute my assertions were these: 'Blockhead, old heretic, the devil made you, I will send you to the devil.' " Frustration gave way to fear when "enemies conspired against me to take away my life, and sometimes, to avoid their hands, my wife did hide me in the roof of the house, covering me with straw." Having become a marked man, he had no choice but to flee to America. He counseled his less notorious fellow Puritans to remain in

1. *New England Historic-Genealogical Register* (Boston, Mass., 1880–), XVI, 279ff. See also *Records,* IV, 2.

Norwich if they possibly could, advising them to "be not dis-
couraged, . . . be chearly . . . have patience . . . abide the
will of God, who worketh all things for the best for you." A
"loving brother in exile persecuted for Christ's verity," Michael
Metcalf would go out alone and unwilling to the savage land
of Massachusetts. He went with his eyes on England, not on
America: "O Norwich! The beauty of my native country—
what shall I say unto thee."

Lives of other early settlers offer other glancing insights into
the society of early Dedham. William Bearstow (alias Barstow,
Beerstowe, Barstawe), for example, was neither as upright
nor as articulate as Metcalf. The Assistants of the colony
ordered him "to be whipped for drunkenness" in 1636. By
the next year he was admitted to Dedham, where he was
assigned a small bachelor's lot. Never a member of the church
or a freeman of the colony, his subsequent land grants were
below the average while his public responsibilities were limited
to duties about the hog-yard in 1637 and menial labor on a
boundary commission of 1641. At one point the town accused
Bearstow of illegally felling timber. He and another defendant
pleaded that it was all a "misunderstanding," but the town found
them guilty, concluding that, "being poor and confessing their
fault," the men should lose only the wood and their labor. The
term "poor" was reserved to describe persons truly destitute,
so it is likely that Bearstow had fallen on hard times. By
1639 he had a wife and child to support, and by 1643 two more
children. As if to compound his problems, the soil of his
eight-acre home lot was found to be stony and he had to ask
compensation from the town in the form of additional land
elsewhere. Sometime after 1643 he removed to Scituate, Massachusetts, selling his land in Dedham shortly thereafter. At
this point he disappears from the record. Perhaps he became a
solid citizen of Scituate, for he did leave some sort of estate at
his death in 1668. It can only be said that for the brief time
he was in Dedham William Bearstow was not a model Puritan

and was not finding the New World a land of milk and honey.[2]

Robert Hinsdell left facts in a trail that will be familiar to Americans as that of the classic pioneer. A pillar of the Dedham church, he was also a member of the first panel of selectmen. He had no trouble in supporting a family which included a wife and six children. In 1651, when an outlying region of the original Dedham grant became the town of Medfield, he moved there and there continued as a respected, prosperous man. Then Hinsdell's life changed abruptly. His attempt to become a merchant went awry, ending in 1663 with the surrender of his ninety-acre farm to the attorney of one Jeremiah Tawke, a London clothier to whom he owed 153 pounds. By this time others of his lands in Medfield had been mortgaged, and in 1671 he sold them all to the wealthy Samuel Shrimpton of Boston. Leaving the scene of his failure, Hinsdell moved out to the frontier town of Hadley, thence to a still more exposed settlement which later became the town of Deerfield. Here he and his family settled; he became a deacon in the church and set about clearing his new lands for agriculture. Four years later, when the Indians rose against the colony, Boston raised an expedition to defend the frontier, but at a place since named Bloody Brook the Indians encircled and overwhelmed the small force. In the massacre Robert Hinsdell and all his sons fell. The long series of moves beginning in England ended there at Bloody Brook in a death that was to become a more usual end for later Americans likewise seeking to begin life anew in the West.[3]

2. *Records of the Court of Assistants of the Colony of Massachusetts Bay, 1630–1692* (3 vols., Boston, Mass., 1904), II, 63; *Records,* III, 28, 31, 46, 60, 62, 79, 86, 96, 106, 110, 151; I, 1, 2, 126; James Savage, *A Genealogical Dictionary of the First Settlers of New England* (4 vols., Boston, Mass., 1860–62), I, 129.

3. *Records,* I, index; II, 13ff; III, 53, 166, 187; Savage, *Genealogical Dictionary,* II, 427; Suffolk County Registry of Deeds, *Grantor* and *Grantee* under "Hinsdell," "Shrimpton"; Massachusetts Historical Society manuscripts under "Hinsdell"; see also Herbert Cornelius Andrews, *Descendants of Robert Hinsdale* (Lombard, Illinois, 1906).

Not everyone who moved from Dedham moved west; Henry
Phillips got fed up and moved back to the city. He had done
well enough since his arrival in 1637, for by 1656 he was a
member of the church, an officer of the militia company, and was
receiving better-than-average dividends of public land. But
the village did not offer him scope for his talents. Angry over
the battle for larger proprietary shares in which he had led a
group of dissatisfied settlers, Phillips moved to Boston without
waiting for the compromise which ultimately restored harmony.
In Boston he showed himself to be a versatile man, becoming
a deacon of the First Church, a deputy to the General Court,
and an enterprising butcher who built a successful business by
catering to the colony's leaders. He died in 1685, after thirty
years of urban life, wealthy and sufficiently well known to merit
mention in Samuel Sewall's famous diary.[4]

Death as well as disappearance from the records might
remove a man from Dedham's history. Edward Alleyn—"Mr."
Alleyn, a title usually reserved for university graduates—began
what might have been a career of considerable distinction. A
pillar of the local church and one of the first panel of selectmen,
he was the town's regular deputy to the General Court following
1638. After numerous services to the community he acquired
the honorary title of "gent." More tangible recognition took
the form of a farm of 350 acres given him by the town. While
active and widely employed in the government of the colony,
Alleyn found time to dabble in schemes for establishing an iron
industry. But in 1642 Edward Alleyn was killed while in Boston

---

4. Here and hereafter, "wealth" means either total estate at death
(from an estate inventory) or taxable estate at a given point in life
(from local tax lists). The two correspond fairly closely, since most of
a man's total estate was taxable. The latter, however, often can only
be expressed in relative terms, because of unknown variables in the
tax-assessment base. *Records*, I, index; II, index; III, 95, 106, 111, 143,
152, 160, 211; IV, 229ff; Savage, *Genealogical Dictionary*, IV, 410;
Suffolk Deeds; *Dedham Historical Register* (14 vols., Dedham, 1890–
1904), III (1892), 158; Suffolk County Court *Files*, no. 894.

on public business, so a career which might have revealed the heights to which a townsman could reach from a base in a rural community was terminated before it had properly begun. Not all the settlers lived to ripe old ages from which they could reflect upon the meaning of their emigration to the New World.[5]

Still, some of them did become virtual patriarchs, relics of the exodus surviving into the days of the third generation. John Gay died in 1688 after half a century in Dedham. His experience described a long descending curve from the respectability of wealth and service into old age and relative poverty. The richest man in town in 1661 and variously a selectman, constable, and member of a county Grand Jury, Gay eased out of public life while his estate slowly tapered down to a mere ninety pounds at his death. Much of the wealth must have gone to his sons, yet other men gave property to their sons while still alive without making themselves near-paupers. And Gay's son, Nathaniel, could not have received too much from his father, since he too died possessed of a small estate. Whatever the reason, it was possible to live so long in the New World and come to so little—not to real poverty, to be sure, but not much above bare subsistence either.[6]

The departures and sad deaths just chronicled may give the impression that Dedham was possessed by a malevolent spirit. Not so. Success was possible, provided vast riches were not the expectation. John Dwight was able to give his son a house and land and still have an estate worth more than 500 pounds on his death in 1660. The usual landmarks of local service and church membership distinguished his career, but more relevant were the large grants of land that went with the distinction of sixteen terms as selectman. Together with judi-

5. *Records*, II, index; III, 36, 42, 44, 52, 53, 55, 67, 73; IV, 289–91; *Records of the Governor and Company of Massachusetts Bay* . . . , I, index under "Alleyn."

6. *Records*, III, 37, 41, 63, 105, 139, 151, 193; IV, 292; V, 41, 70, 99, 156: *New England Historic-Genealogical Register*, IV, 379–80; XI, 112; XXXIII, 45–57.

cious purchases, these grants made Dwight one of the richest townsmen in the years between 1649 and 1660. He passed both his comfortable estate and his prestige on to his son, Timothy, thereby initiating a family line marked by both distinctions.[7]

Eleazer Lusher was the one settler who could have made a fortune had he wished. Within the town his political influence was unmatched, while within the colony he was one of a handful of men who made the vital decisions. His position as deputy and as Assistant brought him into contact with enterprising men from all over New England. Yet Lusher never became overwhelmingly wealthy. His estate of some 500 pounds was less than the estates of several of his village neighbors and only grants of land from town and colony in recognition of his services brought his estate up to this moderate level. He died less wealthy than almost any of his fellow Assistants, never having become a land speculator or merchant as did so many who moved in the higher spheres of power. Whether because of his ignorance or, more likely, because of his restraint, at the end he bequeathed to the distant relatives who survived him only the possessions of a solid local farmer.[8]

These are the outlines of eight lives, the lives of eight Englishmen who came to Dedham early in the seventeenth century. They are varied lives and the possibilities they raise are fascinating. Yet they have limitations. Because the record is meager, their outlines lack many of the meanings which might have been garnered. Only an exceptional life left testimony enough for a full biography and the most exceptional of men often left no clue to their inner thoughts. Moreover, even

7. *Records,* III, 143, 160, index; IV and V, indexes. Also, Benjamin W. Dwight, *The Descendants of John Dwight* (New York, 1874).
8. *Records,* all volumes, indexes; Massachusetts Historical Society card catalog under "Lusher," especially photostat documents dated May 7, 1662, and October 19, 1664; Massachusetts Archives, card catalog index under "Lusher"; Probate Office, Suffolk County, lists wills of most Assistants; *Dedham Historical Register,* II (1891), 130ff.; Suffolk County Deeds.

the sparse details that survive concerning these plain men reveal how difficult it is to base generalizations on the peculiarities of individual lives. For every model Puritan there was a ne'er-do-well; for every pioneer, a butcher; for every patriarch, a man who died prematurely. The very variety which lends fascination also frustrates any attempt to characterize the whole society through individual histories. Ultimately the underlying patterns of society in Dedham can emerge only from a consideration of the dull samenesses which have ever dominated human existence. And what the common features of all lives portray is an isolated, small, stable, homogeneous agricultural community which resembled the rural society of seventeenth-century Europe as much as it resembled the "land of opportunity" dear to the hearts of generations of American students and scholars.[9]

* * *

The overwhelming majority of the settlers came to Dedham to stay. They neither ranged restlessly west nor sought wealth in the developing metropolis of Boston. Most put up temporarily in a nearby town while they looked things over, then moved to Dedham and there initiated a sequence of generations which would intertwine their names with the history of the town for several centuries to come.[10] Because of the stability of the

9. Much of the information that follows is based on collective "biographies" of all of the first fifty men to arrive in town and of slightly over half of the eighty-odd men of a "second generation," which matured between 1665 and 1685. The information is drawn from the *Records,* from the Suffolk County Probate Office Registry of Deeds, and Court Files, from the Massachusetts Archives and the collections of the Massachusetts Historical Society, from manuscript records in the Dedham Historical Society, and from printed sources. Common features have been the focus of the inquiry, and the dominant features are presented here.

10. Though a significant minority, perhaps a third, of the early settlers eventually lived in at least three different New England towns. It is probable that geographic mobility was greater in the first two decades after 1630 than in the entire century thereafter. A detailed

settlers and their posterity, the town became a self-contained social unit, almost hermetically sealed off from the rest of the world. Less than one percent of the adult males in town in a given year would be newcomers, while less than one percent of the adult males would emigrate in a given year. Some of the rare immigrants settled permanently in the town, but others were drifters who did not stay more than a few years and whose departure merely served to raise a little the low level of emigration. Most of the remaining emigrants moved no farther than an adjoining town or "moved" only in the eyes of the law when the distant part of Dedham in which they had always lived was incorporated as a new town. A scattering of officials and servants came and went; young women from nearby towns married into local families while young ladies of Dedham married in turn into the familes of those towns; and some young men left town before reaching the age at which they appeared in the records.[11] Otherwise, hardly anyone stirred in or out. By way of comparison, the only contemporary English villages whose level of mobility is known were consistently more mobile than this American village.[12]

---

analysis of mobility and demographic characteristics in Dedham may be found in K. Lockridge, "The Population of Dedham, Massachusetts, 1636–1736," *Economic History Review*, XIX (1966), 318–44. This article includes data from neighboring Watertown, which confirm the analysis of Dedham.

11. Because of flaws in the early records, the emigration of young men is difficult to trace. An educated guess, based on birth and tax records and genealogical works, would place the level of emigration of males below age twenty-four at between ten and fifteen percent—most probably close to the former. As will be seen, the reluctance of young men to seek opportunity elsewhere was a typical, persistent and highly important feature of Dedham's history; it was a feature found in other towns of New England.

12. See Peter Laslett and John Harrison, "Clayworth and Cogenhoe," *Historical Essays, 1660–1750, Presented to David Ogg* (London, 1963), edited by H. E. Bell and R. L. Ollard. Dedham's decennial rate of continuity was between fifty-six and seventy-six percent, as against forty to fifty percent in Clayworth and Cogenhoe.

In fact, the society of the village was quite narrow and self-centered. The number of family names actually declined from sixty-three in 1648 to fifty-seven in 1688, and an increasing majority of the population belonged to a group of thirty-odd enduring clans who could trace their roots back beyond 1648. Collectively and individually the members of the commune had little to do with outside authorities. They obeyed the law of the colony, but not always. They paid their colony taxes, but the taxes paid for local purposes were usually twice as great. As the town sought to avoid involvement in the courts of the colony, so did each man. The average inhabitant was a plaintiff or defendant in civil proceedings no more than once in his life-time and involvements in criminal proceedings were virtually nonexistent. Nearly all land transactions were small exchanges between Dedham men. Two or three speculators excepted, the seventeenth-century farmer dealt with his neighbors, or with farmers of adjoining towns on those few occasions on which the land he sought was just over the town line.[13]

Seventeenth-century Dedham was a small place, including on the average about 500 souls. It was a little larger than the usual English village and a little smaller than most French villages, but was of a size common to many rural communities in the Atlantic civilization of the time. Yet the town grew steadily throughout the century. The population in 1648 was approximately 400; by 1700, it had risen to nearly 750. Natural increase accounted for the growth, since net immigration was

13. Family data from tax and birth records in *Records,* I, III, IV, V: the law most frequently ignored in the first decades was that requiring registration of land transactions, as a comparison of the town land records in the Dedham Town Hall with the Suffolk County Deeds will show; local expenses included the school costs and the minister's salary, as well as the usual expenses of representation, the meetinghouse, roads, and so forth; see *Records,* III, IV, V; the Index to the Calendar Index of the Suffolk County Court *Files* and the records in the offices of the Clerks of the County and Superior Courts of Suffolk cover in depth certain sample periods on which conclusions have been based; land transactions are found in the sources listed above.

negligible. The significance of the healthy rate of natural
increase can only be appreciated in the light of the stagnation
which characterized the level of population in the villages of
seventeenth-century England and France.[14] If Dedham was
growing steadily while its counterparts in Europe were growing
little if at all, then the fundamental conditions of life in Dedham
must have been better than in Europe.[15]

Better in what way? The obvious explanation that springs
to mind is that the birth rate must have been higher in Dedham
than in seventeenth-century European villages. Surely these
young settlers in a new land were prolific in a way impossible
in the crowded, marginal villages of the Old World? But it
was not so, for the birth rate was about forty births per 1000
population per year—a rate significantly but not remarkably
higher than the birth rates of the villages of Clayworth and
Cogenhoe in England and Crulai in France. Other figures support this judgment. The average intervals between births, the
average number of births per marriage and the average number
of marriages per 1000 population were substantially the same
in Dedham as in these Old World villages. The devastating
statistic which confirms this conclusion is the average age at
marriage, which in Europe ranged around twenty-five years for
women and twenty-seven years for men and in Dedham was
twenty-three for women and twenty-five for men.[16] The differ-

14. Again, see Lockridge, "The Population of Dedham." European
figures are drawn from J. D. Chambers, *The Vale of Trent, 1670–1800*
(London, 1957), E. Hobsbawm, "The Crisis of the Seventeenth Century,"
Past and Present, nos. 5 and 6 (1954), Laslett and Harrison, "Clayworth
and Cogenhoe," and Pierre Goubert, *Beauvais et les Beauvaisis de 1600
à 1730* (2 vols., Paris, 1958).

15. Dedham's rate and pace of growth closely parallel those of
Massachusetts as a whole, thus making it likely that the town's demographic structure was typical of this part of the New World and that
the advantages it enjoyed were typically "American" advantages. See
Lockridge, "The Population of Dedham."

16. European sources as above, plus A. Drake, "An Elementary
Exercise in Parish Register Demography," *Economic History Review,*

ence in female marriage ages argues for a slightly higher birth rate in Dedham—since the younger women marry, the longer they are "eligible" to have children and the shorter the part of their fertile span that is wasted—but similarity is the main point. And, whether twenty-five or twenty-seven, the middle twenties are a late time for a man to begin married life. In a patronizing assumption of New World superiority, American demographers have commented sadly on the unfortunate conditions that kept European men from acquiring the wherewithal to support a family until they were nearly thirty. Their assumption was wrong, because in Dedham just as in Crulai or Clayworth a man did not find opportunity so plentiful that he could marry as young as he chose.

A great part of Dedham's steady growth and corresponding natural advantages over European villages must be explained through a lower death rate. At most, there were twenty-seven deaths per 1000 per year as against rates of thirty to forty and higher in Europe. Much of the difference can probably be ascribed to such long-range causes as better diet or better housing, conditions which acted year in and year out to prolong the lives of older persons and to ensure that more infants survived the critical days following birth. A more readily identifiable difference lay in the relative absence of short-range demographic "crises" in Dedham. In Europe, particularly in France, famines and plagues struck repeatedly. Often coming in clusters within a ten or twenty-year period, these disasters could wipe out a tenth, a quarter, a half or more of the population of a village. Crises were so severe in some French villages that they created "echoes," periods of low births a generation apart reflecting the initial crisis period of deaths and delayed marriages: fewer children were born or survived birth during a crisis; on reaching maturity their generation had fewer persons

---

XIV (1962), 427, and Louis Henry and Etienne Gautier, *La Population de Crulai, Paroisse Normande* (Paris, 1958).

available for marriage; a generation with fewer marriages had fewer children; and so it went until circumstances smoothed out the echoing flaw over a period of three or four generations. Dedham went through well over a half century without experiencing a single crisis which removed as much as ten percent of its population within a two-year span. For some reason this New World village was spared at least the worst ravages of disease, famine, and climate, effects all too familiar to rural Europeans of the time.[17] It would be foolish to launch out in Jeffersonian praises of the benefits of benevolent nature in a new land free from the depravities of Europe, yet it is clear that the new land had some material gifts to offer and freedoms to bestow other than the freedom from Anglican persecution.

The town's insulation from the forces of nature had other results. Dedham paralleled Crulai in its seasons of birth, conceptions reaching a peak in the spring and descending to a low in the autumn. But in the New World town the difference between the month of highest conceptions and the month of lowest conceptions was lower than in Crulai. Children were being conceived throughout the year with distinctly less regard for the natural forces—climate, food, labor, whatever—which tended to impose a cyclic yearly pattern of conception on all the rural societies of the world.[18]

Yet in other ways nature did impose itself on human life in Dedham in just the same way and often as severely as in Europe. The similarities in birth rates and marriage ages bear witness to this truth, as does the parallel timing of the yearly cycle of conception. Then too, this town had its severe years; 1675–76 saw twenty-five deaths occur in Dedham. Several of the twenty-five were killed fighting in the same Indian war (King Philip's War) that had resulted in Robert Hinsdell's death, but most died of age and disease in the long season of alarms and

17. Lockridge, "Population of Dedham," and Goubert, *Beauvais.*
18. Lockridge, "Population of Dedham," and Henry and Gautier, *Crulai.*

excursions that accompanied the war. And year in and year
out the seasons of death in Dedham were the same as in the
European villages. In all, deaths occurred most frequently
in the winter months, when cold, poor diet, and confinement
combined to weaken the strong and kill the weak. No insulation
from nature blessed Dedham with a reduction in the toll of
deaths that mounted to a peak every December, January,
February.[19]

The economy was agricultural. Men called themselves "yeoman" or "husbandman" as any farmer called himself in England.
There was always a miller or two, a blacksmith, a cordwainer or
other artisan in the town to supply the specialized needs of the
economy, but easily eighty-five percent of the male inhabitants
characterized themselves as farmers and most of the rest
derived the greater part of their support from the land.[20] It
was an unspecialized agriculture which they practiced, devoted
largely to mere subsistence, and was very like the agriculture
practiced in many sections of rural England. The same oaken
tubs full of the same crops (peas, barley, wheat, rye, oats, hay,
fruit)[21] from fields of similar sizes rested in identical rooms in
matching houses of farmers who achieved equal if modest prosperity and participated in like rural offices (poundkeeper, fenceviewer, hogreeve) in Dedham as in England.[22]

What exactly might a farmer possess? His land aside, he
would own essentially the possessions of an English yeoman
farmer: within his house of two to eight rooms were a few beds,
chests and chairs, a little pewter or silver, perhaps two changes

19. See Footnote 18.
20. Based on wills and inventories in the Suffolk County Probate
Office and on occupational labels in documents in the Suffolk County
Registry of Deeds.
21. Indian corn excepted.
22. See Mildred Campbell, *The English Yeoman under Elizabeth
and the Early Stuarts* (New Haven, Conn., 1942); W. G. Hoskins,
*The Midland Peasant, The Economic and Social Structure of a Leicester-
shire Village* (London, 1957); and A. N. Garvan, *Architecture and
Town Planning in Colonial Connecticut* (New Haven, Conn., 1951).

of clothing and a good suit and cloak, a Bible, sometimes with commentaries thereon; outside was a barn or lean-to containing agricultural tools, a cart, bins, bowls, pots and pans, a few bushels of each of the staple crops, and finally a horse or two, several cattle and five or six each of sheep and swine. His whole estate would come to between 200 and 400 pounds Massachusetts currency.

No crop became a cash crop grown in quantity at the expense of others. The agricultural surpluses listed in the inventories varied with the season but were always small and distributed among three or four crops. This held for livestock as well. John Allin died in possession of twenty-eight sheep in 1671, John Bacon of twenty-four cattle in 1683, but these relatively modest herds were the height of acquisition in an economy in which specialized entrepreneurial farming was unknown. The farmers doubtless traded small quantities of grain, wood, beef and hides in nearby Boston in order to obtain the few manufactured necessities that were beyond their means to produce. Still, the message of the inventories of their estates is unmistakable: no single crop or animal dominated the village economy, and the farmers died without leaving the multiplicity of debts or credits with Boston merchants which would have resulted from a more developed commercial relationship.[23]

Yet this simple subsistence economy was also an economy of abundance, for there was an incomparable abundance of land. To be sure, soil was often poor; even free public land grants had to be surveyed at some expense; a man's grant might be distant from his home; and if land was cheap to buy that was in part because it was wilderness land that would take years of backbreaking labor to clear. Yet there was land.

23. As might be supposed, wealth came from within the town. No Dedham men drew a majority of their wealth from outside sources. Within Dedham, prices remained fairly stable throughout the second half of the seventeenth century. Again, the relevant documents are in the Suffolk County Probate Office in Boston.

Privately owned land cost shillings an acre instead of pounds an acre as in England, and most townships were giving it away free. In Dedham, the conservatism of the town's early land policy did not last forever. No more than 3000 acres had been allotted in the first twenty years, but in the next twelve years over 15,000 acres were divided among the proprietors. A man who lived in the town for any twenty-five year span between 1636 and 1686 received between fifty and 500 acres from the town, 150 acres on the average.[24] This was by no means a farmstead beyond the wildest dreams of a successful English yeoman, but it meant security for the whole society of the village since it made every man a potential yeoman, a status enjoyed by only a fortunate minority of the English rural populace. It was a promise to every man's posterity, guaranteeing that the next generation would inherit the raw material of self-support. Even a younger son of a less than distinguished settler could expect a patrimony which would keep him from having to rent land or work for another man or beg in the streets.

The leaders of the colony reflected a general awareness of the unique abundance of the New World in the novel inheritance law they created. In England, the lands of a man who left no will would go to his eldest son under the law of primogeniture, whose aim was to prevent the fragmentation of holdings which would follow from a division among all the sons. This law arose from a mentality of scarcity. It left the landless younger sons to fend for themselves. In New England the law provided for the division of the whole estate among all the children of the deceased. Why turn younger sons out on the society without land or perhaps daughters without a decent

24. Land grants are in *Records*, III, IV, V and in manuscripts in the Dedham Town Hall. For English comparisons see Campbell, *English Yeoman*, Hoskins, *The Midland Peasant*, H. J. Habakkuk, "English Landownership, 1680–1740," *Economic History Review*, X(1940), 14, and Martha Jane Ellis, "Halifax Parish, 1558–1640" (Ph.D. dissertation, Radcliffe-Harvard, 1958).

dowry, why invite social disorder, when there was enough to provide for all? [25] The plentitude of land, the novel intestacy law, and the benevolent practices of those yeomen who did leave wills combined in New England to offer the entire second generation the promise of prosperity within the familiar social framework of the village in which their fathers had settled. It was a deeply satisfying prospect to men whose homeland had contained a fair share of wandering laborers, struggling apprentices, and paupers.

As might be expected, the society of the town was rather homogeneous. The circumstances of the emigration had fostered a certain homogeneity from the very beginning, for no noblemen or true English gentlemen settled in Dedham, while the few servants among the founders soon became independent yeomen. Though the social policy of the founders had embraced a degree of social differentiation by recognizing "rank and quality" earned in England as the basis for larger allotments of land in the New World, in fact the settlers of appreciable "rank and quality" were few, they did not receive extremely large bonuses of land as a result of their distinction, and they had to compete for allotments with men who met the more practical standards for extra land—such as skill in farming or large familes. Above all, the abundance of land and the simplicity of the economy mitigated against the rapid evolution of radical social differences among the middle-class Englishmen who settled the town. Impoverished "laborers" hardly existed in this society of abundant land. Servants amounted to less than five percent of the population and were nearly all either captive Indians, Negro slaves (of whom there were very few), or young children serving in another family as part of their upbringing.[26] The

25. Charles M. Andrews, *The Connecticut Intestacy Law* (Connecticut Tercentenary Pamphlet, New Haven, Conn., 1933); George L. Haskins, *Law and Authority in Early Massachusetts;* Richard B. Morris, *Studies in the History of American Law* (New York, 1930).

26. *Records,* V, 121–22 contains a census of servants. The Probate

occasional "poor" individual was usually a sick widow or an orphan, or an improvident half-wit. On the other hand men who came to be known as "gentleman" were even more rare and had earned their titles through long and distinguished public service. The more wealthy farmers—even those of families with original pretensions to a little "rank and quality" and who were called on to serve as selectmen not infrequently—continued to refer to themselves as yeomen, which they were. They might have had a little more wealth and distinction than the average farmer, but their estates were identical in structure to those of men with half as much wealth and their style of life was correspondingly similar—a style in which every man toiled on his own lands. While they no doubt expected and certainly were given respect, they retained a good measure of Puritan honesty about their social position and refused to take titles of gentility.

The distribution of taxable wealth reflected the *de facto* homogeneity of the economy and the society. The five percent of men who paid the highest taxes controlled but fifteen percent of the taxable wealth in Dedham. This degree of concentration implied a certain hierarchy of wealth within the town, but was far more equitable than the concentration of wealth in the hands of the few which came to prevail in seventeenth-century Boston. In this developing commercial center the richest five percent of men controlled twenty-five percent of the wealth. At the bottom of the social spectrum, the lowest twenty percent of men owned eight percent of the taxable wealth in Dedham as against three percent of the wealth in Boston.

So the cheapness of land and the low level of the subsistence economy had done much to keep the distribution of wealth relatively even and the spectrum of social rank narrow, thereby making it easier for the town's leaders to maintain a social

---

Records and Deeds for Suffolk County include occupational and honorary titles and yield information on estates, landholdings, etc. Millers, who did consistently well, seem to have had the only "gimmick" that led to wealth.

harmony predicated on a judicious blending of collective interest with a moderate degree of hierarchy. If anything, it had been necessary to emphasize the latter just a little here and there, to prevent its being swallowed in the former. The founders of Boston faced an opposite problem, as its distribution of wealth indicates, and the brief history of the utopian impulse in that city showed the deadly effects of excessive concentration of wealth resulting from rapid economic development.[27]

In sum, what kind of life did such a society offer? It certainly offered a man the opportunity to live a long life on his own land among a group of equals and near-equals. But this appealing prospect was tempered by the inherent conservatism of the social environment. To follow the fortunes of a young man from year to year is to perceive the bonds which knit him to his society and his society to the special world of all peasant villages. He could expect to be a farmer, like his father. He would stay in the village, for his father's death held out the promise of land. It would take time, for almost any farmer who passed forty would live to be sixty before dying. A son might be given lands while the patriarch was still alive, but woe unto him who angered his father! (There was the story of one father who cut his second son out of his will because he dared to disobey his father's order to grow barley on the five acres given him to test his sense of the land.) Of course a youth could strike out on his own within the town . . . if he could find a way to earn money, that is, and if his father would let him, since a man was not really free of paternal discipline

27. The top ten percent of Dedham taxpayers controlled twenty-five percent of the taxable wealth. Figures are drawn from *Records,* III, IV, V, all tax lists. For comparative figures for Boston, see James A. Henretta, "Economic Development and Social Structure in Colonial Boston," *William and Mary Quarterly,* XXII (1965), 75–92. For a typology based on the distribution of wealth in the towns of late eighteenth-century America, see Jackson T. Main, *The Social Structure of Revolutionary America* (Princeton, N.J., 1965). Also, see chapter 8. The fate of Boston's utopian impulse is chronicled in Darrett B. Rutman, *Winthrop's Boston* (Chapel Hill, N.C., 1965).

until he reached the voting age of twenty-four. But at last the day would come when his inheritance finally cleared the courts. Even if his father had been well off, it might not be much, by the time the older brothers got their shares and part of the estate was set aside for the use of the widow. Still, it would do for a start, and now, at the age of twenty-five or twenty-six, he could marry and begin a family. The land would take some clearing and it was sometimes thin soil such as could drive a man to other employment if other were to be had, but it was his land and better than nothing. Twenty or thirty years of hard work aided by the labor of his own sons might enable the farmer to save enough to buy a little extra land, and dividends of public land would further swell his holdings. By now in his late forties himself, he might have earned enough respect to be elected selectman. But by now he was nearly an old man, left to husband his estate for the sons who were in their turn anticipating their father's will. At least he had had the satisfaction of progressing as well as most: no one had passed him by on the way to fabulous riches, nor would any catastrophe be likely to wipe out his holdings.[28] He depended on no city man or foreigner for his income, and, although his home could be easily destroyed by fire, it could as easily be rebuilt out of local materials with the help of his neighbors. It would have been a good enough life, though rather hard and lonely since his wife and youngest child had died.

* * *

So on the one hand it was unmistakably an "American" society. The seemingly unending potentialities of the virgin lands which surrounded Dedham had their due effects on the

28. This is based on sources previously cited, particularly on an analysis of the rate of upward and downward economic mobility of forty members of the second generation whose names occur on the tax lists in *Records,* IV, V, VI (1706–1736), and on a study of inheritance customs as evinced in the wills of seventeenth-century townsmen in the Suffolk County Probate Office.

life of every man, helping to prolong that life and opening to it possibilities unthinkable for the Everyman of England. The absence of a privileged aristocracy and of the masses of the poor left the community free of the drastic human inequalities which plagued European society. Life was indeed better than in England and far removed from the sometimes appalling conditions of France under the old regime.[29]

But the America of social diversity and ideological pluralism was never more distant. If the society was one of opportunity, it was the continually present opportunity to take up land and become another subsistence farmer. No social or industrial revolution was taking place, increasing social opportunity by altering its distribution in the society or by opening new avenues of upward mobility. And the equality of the society was nothing less than the equality of economic interests which lies at the heart, not of modern pluralistic democracy, but of Marxist-Leninist democracy. One class, one interest, one mind—how can there help but be voluntary unanimity within such a society? As it was to have been yet never was and never could be with Marx's hopelessly idealized industrial proletariat, so to a remarkable degree, it really was with the farmers of the Dedham commune.

Furthermore, an awareness of the diverse possibilities of rural society in seventeenth-century Europe can serve as a needed corrective for the evidence of uniquely American opportunity in Dedham. Europe included many nations, each with many regions. Here and there in the interstices of Old World society can be found villages whose way of life resembled that of "American" Dedham. The English village of Wilston Magna

29. Indirect support for the idea of a "spectrum" of social conditions ranging from France to America may be found in the works previously cited and in Pierre Goubert, "The French Peasantry of the Seventeenth Century: A Regional Example," *Past and Present,* no. 10 (1956), 55–77.

is one example. By the seventeenth century there were no lords of the manor in this village, all having sold out to peasant proprietors. Many families owned land, farming areas of twenty to forty acres for the most part, areas comparable to those actually under cultivation in early Dedham. It was "a solid community of middling size farmers, . . . with no overshadowing family at the top, ..." Not an isolated case, the English village was "representative of a considerable number of midland villages where a substantial body of peasant proprietors still kept their hold on the land." [30]

If some Old World villages offered many of the beneficial conditions found in New World Dedham, it is even more true that New World Dedham embodied many of the traditional conditions found in most Old World villages. Dedham, Clayworth, and Crulai were three small agricultural villages which existed in an age long before modern medicine, scientific farming, and industrial productivity. Winter was to be feared in each of them, harvests were a gamble that kept men aware of Providence, diseases arose and subsided outside of all human control and infants died in numbers that would shock us today. A man ready to marry did not just go out and get a job; he prepared a farm of his own or else made sure he could expect to inherit the family home and acres. A person who lived to seventy, a normal lifespan in our century, found that he was one of the few survivors of his generation. Collectively, a town was likely to retain its customs and peculiarities for a long time. The few newcomers admitted each year soon adopted the ways found comfortable by the clansmen of the town for generations past. Few left town, for the ways of the community were reassuringly familiar. Most men showed the typical peasant's satisfaction with the *status quo:* It worked for his father and for his father before him, why tinker with success? Why, especially when it

---

30. W. G. Hoskins, *The Midland Peasant,* 143–44.

could be dangerous? Some of Dedham's customs may have been unique, but chances are they soon became as unthinkingly rigid as any in Europe. It could hardly have been otherwise in a society that in so many ways still followed the ancient, universal patterns of rural life.

5

Decline

~~~~~~

DEDHAM'S AGE of utopian communalism contained within itself the seeds of change, just as later the age in which change would become the dominant theme of the town's history would contain in turn the continuing impulse of the past.

As any Puritan would have been the first to admit, the impulse toward perfection is doomed to failure. Crippled by original sin, man's reason cannot discern the nature of God's plan for the universe. Still less can human reason put into practice and maintain whatever chimera of social perfection it happens to light upon. This theory was never better illustrated than in the case of earliest Dedham. Though no violent changes disturbed the even tenor of village life, the overriding utopian concern gradually evaporated. All the covenants, catechisms, and bylaws in the world could not have stopped the process, for at its heart lay the everlasting inability of human nature to satisfy its own recurring hunger for the absolute. By the end of the first half-century, the policies of perfection no longer held sway.

*   *   *

The process of decline began with the beginning of the community. Even as town and church wrote their covenants and set about putting their principles into practice, imperfections arose. What Plato called "the recalcitrance of the medium" made itself felt in seemingly trival ways: "Contentment" was renamed "Dedham" by an unimaginative General Court; Thomas Cakebread, a skilled miller, decided not to add his skills to the new community; the respected and learned John Phillips was unable to join the church as its first minister. But as the years passed, trival disappointments were replaced by imperfections of ever larger consequence until at last the failings had so eroded the successes that the integral utopian spirit could no longer be said to exist.

A little of the intended unity was sacrificed as early as 1639, when the meeting of all townsmen delegated its powers to the selectmen. Perhaps "the general meeting of so many men" *had* "wasted much time," but it had also enabled every townsman to participate directly in every decision. Now the pure consensual unity of the founders would disappear and most decisions would pass into the hands of a few leaders—all in the name of efficiency.

It had been the town's practice to set aside six days out of each year for work on the highways and to require each man to work any four of the six days. On the appointed day, the townsmen would work shoulder-to-shoulder until the roads were once again in good repair. But here, too, the communal ideal fell short when an early bylaw allowed a man to hire a substitute. Instead of displaying in their soiled hands the evidence of a common obligation, thenceforth the more successful townsmen could use their wealth to lift themselves above the herd. Eventually, a similar procedure would allow the well-off to buy themselves out of their turn at the burdensome office of constable. By the terms of the Covenant all townsmen were equally privileged and equally bound, but money soon made some more equal than others.[1]

By the 1650's circumstances had begun to create a series of privileged subcorporations within the community, further

1. *Records,* III, 8, and index under "Highways". For the constable issue, see the notebook of Jeremiah Fisher, Justice of the Peace, among the manuscripts in the Dedham Historical Society.

undermining the total unity envisioned in the Covenant. The tapering off of new memberships in the church which began in these years had led by 1670 to a congregation which excluded a majority of the townsmen. The formal proprietorship of the town lands was shared by nearly all townsmen at the inception of that institution in 1656, but thereafter new arrivals unable to purchase shares from an existing proprietor were shut out of this privilege. The town corporation itself ceased to be identical with the community since, after about 1660, new arrivals were not always invited to sign the Covenant. Thus, a group of six or eight Scotsmen settled in Dedham in the 1660's without subscribing to the pact. They were not warned out; they paid taxes, worked and even married in the community just as did any townsman; but they were by implication second-class citizens.[2] The irony in all of this is that the founders' drive for perfection carried the seeds of its own failure. Their perfect church had the imperfection of excluding some townsmen from its sacraments, while their perfect town excluded some of its inhabitants from the proprietorship and from its Covenant. It could not be helped.

2. The development of these subcorporations, particularly that of the proprietorship, could be seen as a first step in the transition from what anthropologists would label a "semiegalitarian, semirank" society into a full "rank" society and further into a "stratified" society. The economic and social developments to be discussed in chapter eight completed this development and left the community almost fully "stratified" in the technical sense. See Morton H. Fried, "On the Evolution of Social Stratification and the State," in *Culture in History,* S. Diamond, ed. (New York, 1960). This process toward stratification was a factor in the decline of the closed corporate community, for such a community is based above all on shared risks, shared obligations, and shared rewards, all of which rank and above all stratification tend to erode. See Eric Wolf, "Closed Corporate Peasant Communities in Mesoamerica and Central Java," *Southwestern Journal of Anthropology,* XIII (Spring, 1957), 1–18. Indeed, as will be seen in the second section of this book, every one of the structural and ideological dilemmas Dedham faced was typical of those which face any closed corporate peasant community, and Dedham's disintegration followed more or less the pattern to be expected in such cases.

If the corporate unity of the village was slowly eroding, so was its physical coherence. The common field system began disintegrating almost from the day of its inception. Already in the 1640's the town permitted men to "fence their lots in particular" and presumably to grow in these lots whatever crops they wished. By the 1670's it had become usual for men to take up both special "convenience grants" and their usual shares of each new dividend in locations as close as possible to their existing lots, practices which aided the consolidation of individual holdings. The process encouraged by public policy was completed by private transactions, for an active market in small parcels of land soon emerged, a market in which most farmers sought to sell distant lands and buy lands closer to their main holdings. The net result was the coalescence of private farms. From here, it would be but two short steps for farmers whose holdings were centered in outlying areas to move their barns and then their houses from the village out to their lands. As of 1686 few seem to have taken these steps, but the way had been prepared and the days of a society totally enclosed by the village were numbered. In any event the common-field system was gone, taking with it the common decisions and the frequent encounters of every farmer with his fellows which it entailed.[3]

The evidences of increasing imperfection were not always so subtle. After twenty years several overt breaches appeared in the rule of love. Though each was a transient episode and was resolved within the town as the Covenant had prescribed, in fact and in implication each was rather more serious than the sorts of disagreements forseen in the Covenant. The 1656 demand of some disgruntled settlers, led by Henry Phillips, for larger shares in the proprietorship, and the sudden rejection in 1660 of the powers and members of the board of selectmen

3. *Records,* III, 77, 101; IV, 22, 85; also manuscript land records in the Dedham Town Hall and wills and inventories in the Suffolk County Probate Office.

by a discontented majority of townsmen, had each in its own way threatened to stretch the policy of consensus beyond its limits. As far as Phillips himself was concerned, those limits had been passed, for he had gone off to Boston in a fit of anger. Moreover, at one point Phillips and his friends had gone so far as to bring their cause to the attention of the General Court, thereby setting an unhealthy precedent of appeal to higher authorities. Had that precedent become a general practice, the whole mechanism of the Covenant might have collapsed forthwith. The political contretemps of 1660 was no less disturbing in its implications. Had the total rejection of authority which it embodied become characteristic, the orderly society of the Covenant might have dissolved into chaos. Amidst their self-congratulations on having eased these episodes into quick and peaceful resolutions, the leaders of the town might have pondered the potential dangers that time was uncovering.

The most notable failure of the policy of peace was external rather than internal. From 1651 to 1665 and sporadically thereafter, Dedham carried on a stubborn legal battle against the Christian Indians of neighboring Natick.[4] At issue was a section of land along the Charles River. The Indians, who were cultivating the land even though it fell within the bounds of the Dedham grant, made the dubious claim that an "agreement" with the Dedham townsmen gave them the right to farm there. But the Indians' leader, the Reverend John Eliot, rested his case most heavily on the moral issue of his followers' need of land. Virtually alone among all the Europeans who pledged themselves to convert the heathen, Eliot had kept his pledge, winning many of the local Indians over to Christianity and to a stable, agricultural life. It now seemed that Eliot had been too successful, for the very increase in the numbers of his converts had created a demand for farmland which in turn had brought on the encroachment on Dedham's territory. Should

4. Many of the relevant documents can be found reprinted in *Records,* IV, Appendix.

the mere letter of the law now choke off his holy enterprise? Eliot's answer was "No." But Dedham's answer was "Yes." Legal right was in fact with the townsmen and they would have their rights. Yet no amount of legal right could have justified the deceptions, retaliations, and lasting bitterness which characterized Dedham's role in the case. The town did not even have the good grace to drop the issue once the General Court had imposed a compromise by which the "praying Indians" got some of the land and Dedham received compensation elsewhere. The townsmen continued to harass their neighbors with petty accusations. When good land was at stake and the other party was "savage," the spirit of the Covenant could be set aside. But once set aside, could it be taken up again without having lost some of its power?

Still, the town held the line against disappointment, dispersion, and occasional imperfection as long as its original leadership remained intact. Not until the 1670's and 1680's, when the great men of local politics had died or left office, did the decline become obvious. Peter Woodward left office in 1670; Eleazer Lusher and Joshua Fisher died in 1672; Timothy Dwight served only rarely after ending a string of nine consecutive terms as selectman in 1681; and Daniel Fisher died in 1683.[5] Young men in the days when the Covenant was written, several of these men had been among those who had first agreed upon the principles which it embodied, and all had entered office at a time when the policies of perfection were in full force. Several were also founders of the church. Their long service and the respect in which they came to be held had virtually guaranteed the community against a loss of purpose. As they and their compatriots began to disappear the policies they had wielded fell into disuse.

The bylaws restricting the presence of strangers in the town were not often applied after 1675. Mediators and arbi-

5. See Lockridge and Kreider, "The Evolution of Massachusetts Town Government" for a more detailed analysis of this transition and of a remarkably similar transition in neighboring Watertown.

trators were asked less and less often to settle disputes, while evidence of concern for the "convenience" of men with problems was ever less apparent and the many small manifestations of a "loving spirit" came to be conspicuous by their absence. Evidence of dissent began to appear in the records, first in the form of challenges to the selectmen's arranging of the seating in the meetinghouse, then as requests that dissenting votes in town meetings be counted and recorded. By 1686 such small sins of omission and commission had destroyed much of the overt utopianism of the founders. The end of the age of peace was epitomized in the list of duties assigned to the newly created office of town treasurer in 1687: "to make demand, sue . . . according to law . . . and to receive moneys from the inhabitants to carry on such suits at law, or matters of trouble." [6]

Men were not entirely unaware of what was happening to their communal ideal. In at least one instance the loss of voluntary unity was accompanied by an agonizing consciousness of failure. The minister's salary had been raised by private contribution until shortly before the death of John Allin in 1671. But once Allin became old and infirm and it became necessary to hire visiting ministers to help fill his post, contributions began to lag. In 1670, "divers of the inhabitants coming this day to the selectmen and moved that some care might be taken that our reverend Pastor might have his salary yearly paid." From this day forward the collection of the minister's salary was a running problem of the town, one which exemplified the weakness of the flesh in the face of the pecuniary demands of the spirit.

They tried to preserve the old way at first:

In reference to the present way of contribution in each Lord's day, these two questions were put. One: whether a proportion shall be made wherein each shall be assessed what he is to pay and

6. For examples, see *Records,* V, 19, 121, 183. The quotation is from V, 200.

a committee chosen to make that proportion accordingly. Voted in the negative. Two: whether, in consideration of what have been spoken from scripture and argument referring to the duty and rule of [voluntary] contribution as to conscience . . . in the sight and fear of God, the case may not at present be left in the same way of contribution that at present and for some time past we have practiced, hoping that every man will endeavour to keep a good conscience therein, at least for trial. The vote passed in the affirmative to this second question by general consent.[7]

But by 1672 the town was forced to adopt the "proportion" scheme which they had at first rejected, since some men continued to ignore the dictates of God and good conscience. Henceforth each man would be responsible for a definite proportion of the minister's salary, though it was up to him to contribute this from Sunday to Sunday and he could add to it as he pleased. Not quite a compulsory tax yet no longer the old free personal offering, this arrangement represented a major breach in the voluntaristic ideology of the community. It was only the beginning.

The town struggled against the inevitable for the next thirty years. Though Allin's successor, William Adams, complained frequently of arrears, the town refused to guarantee his salary by turning its "collection by proportion" into an actual tax. They would assign each man his due share and hope that either shame or conscience would lead him to pay it, but they would not send the constable around with a warrant if he did not pay. When Joseph Belcher succeeded to the Dedham pulpit, he even made an attempt to restore the collection of most of his salary to a purely private basis. Even though the burden of the minister's salary on the individual was decreasing as the number of townsmen rose faster than the value of the salary, Belcher's attempt failed. And the "proportion" system to which the town then reverted proved itself as inadequate under Belcher as it had been under Adams. By 1704 all fiction of voluntarism was discarded. After this date it became the practice of the town

7. *Records*, IV, 204, 214.

to assign arrears on the proportions to the constables for collection. The euphemistic "proportion" came to be called what it in fact had become, a "rate," an ordinary tax.[8] If a man did not pay, he would become subject to the penalties of the law. The town abandoned its idealistic free contributions reluctantly, but abandon them it did, and in abandoning them it left behind another part of the old communal synthesis.

More strictly religious problems also arose to plague the community. Though it never caused an explosion of resentment, the runaway exclusiveness of the congregation had a fanatical tinge that did not compare well with the humility of the founders. It was possible to be too true to their doctrines, to cling to the technical point of a church of saints at the expense of the original impulse toward love and consensus. Twice after 1671 the town had paid the price of the congregation's stubbornness by having to do without a settled minister for long periods. Was it a reasonable price? Had the covenants of either church or town foreseen that this would happen?

Not even the exaggerated exclusiveness which was the last remnant of the utopian impulse survived much beyond 1686. Within five years thereafter the congregation was forced to abandon its desperate insistence on a church of saints and to accept the inevitable compromise of the Half-Way Covenant. In the same years the town was required to come to terms with changes which it, in turn, regarded as infringements on its purity. Like most of their fellow colonists, the men of Dedham had become increasingly fearful under the constant threat of interference from England. By the 1680's this fear had reached the proportions of a mania. Blind resistance to any assertion of Crown power was the order of the day. Most colonists were convinced that the original Charter of 1629 and the covenant with God which it represented must be kept intact at all costs and that negotiations with the English authorities could only mean compromise, a compromise with corruption which would

8. *Records,* V, VI, indexes under "constable," "minister's salary," "arrears," "Adams," and "Belcher."

surely invite the wrath of God. The Crown's reaction was to
withdraw the old charter and impose a Royal government
headed by Sir Edmund Andros. But he was overthrown by
the people of Massachusetts as soon as it became known that
the Glorious Revolution of 1689 had removed his master, James
II, from the throne. The hatred of the "foreign" regime was
so great in Dedham that the townsmen followed up Andros'
fall by repudiating every selectman who had served during the
years of his rule. Eight men with a total of over fifty years'
experience served from 1687 to 1689, and though all lived for
some time thereafter, only one ever again served as selectman
and he only for a single term. In their places the town put
five young men with a collective total of but two years' experience, all of whom promptly pledged support to the local
revolution and the old charter. Such excesses of Puritan
patriotism could not alter the course of history, however, and
William III, James' successor, imposed a compromise in the
form of the Charter of 1691. Under its terms the Charter of
1629 became a dead letter, a Royal governor replaced the
locally chosen governor of former times, and writs ran in the
name of the King of England. By the 1690's Dedham, with
the rest of Massachusetts, had been required to accept the reality
of some degree of English control. There was no longer any
point in local purges in the name of political purity.[9]

* * *

The waning of the explicit social synthesis of the Dedham
Covenant was a subtle thing, as subtle yet as pervasive as the
synthesis itself. There had been no dramatic social upheaval

9. *Records,* I, V, especially 203; see also *Massachusetts Archives,*
CVII; and Viola Barnes, *The Dominion of New England* (New Haven,
Conn., 1923). There is a distant possibility that the Dedham electoral
purge of 1689 also involved a revolt of youth against the limited
suffrage and the rule of their elders. If this is so, it may be no
accident that the end of exclusiveness in the church came only two
years thereafter.

brought on by irresistable material forces, nor had a cathartic moral crisis replaced the old synthesis with a new. The village remained a small, slowly growing community with traditional views and unchanging institutions. It was just that the utopian aura was gone. Something almost intangible had happened, then, and for almost inscrutable reasons. The townsmen might as well have attributed the change to a dozen small shifts of circumstance as to the gradually waning spiritual energies which, at times, they seemed to think were at fault.[10] Although, most likely, they simply subsumed all causes under the wrath of a truly inscrutable God who could punish men both by altering their circumstances and by sapping their faith. That was cause enough. But, whether the forces of nature, the fallability of the human spirit, or the wrath of God was most responsible, the fact is that something most certainly had happened. By 1686, the Covenant was no longer enforced and would never again be the guide for every policy and every

10. Anthropologists would place the weight of causation solely on shifting material circumstances—such as growth, immigration, and the evolution of a status hierarchy—rather than deal with anything so intangible as a "waning of spiritual energy." In their view, the latter is the result of the former, an effect rather than a cause. To the extent that this is true, the "decline" of the utopian impulse in Dedham in the later seventeenth century was merely the first phase of a typical process of material change which, in more obvious ways, was shortly to cause more overt changes in the life of the town (see note 3, above, and chapters 6, 7, 8). But, if so, it was a somewhat diffuse phase, both in its causes and in its effects. And, for those who wish to leave room for the dark night of the soul, the fact is that, at least in the case of the decline of voluntary support of the ministry, the townsmen themselves seem to have believed that the problem was purely one of weakening spiritual energy. Surely such a thing does happen, and is one part of the process by which the more extreme examples of utopian corporate communities loose their coherence. Indeed, it may be that in Dedham it was the decline of spiritual resolve which permitted such material changes as the evolution of certain of the subcorporations and the lapse of the common field system to occur. If this was the case, then the loss of resolve is a distinct preliminary phase in the dissolution of at least this closed corporate community, and perhaps of others.

action. The harmonious society so painstakingly built under its influence no longer existed in all its original integrity.

The only satisfaction the townsmen could have salvaged was that it all appeared to have happened according to strict Puritan theory. In "A Modell of Christian Charity," John Winthrop had predicated the successful application of Christian love upon the existence of a large majority of saints, who were able to sustain that love because they had received God's restoring grace. In Dedham, when the saints dwindled and died away, the rule of love dwindled and died with them. In this sense, too, the New England preachers of the 1670's and 80's could take some satisfaction in being right. Their famous laments over the decline of the spirit of the founders were justified by events in Dedham. Small wonder the wrath of God was now descending.

Perhaps, in retrospect, there is another satisfaction to be gained. Though all too short from the point of view of a Puritan divine, the life of the utopian commune had been longer than anyone had a right to expect. Created in the midst of a howling wilderness, it had remained essentially intact well into the lifetime of the second generation. It has been said that America is the place where utopias are put into practice . . . and found impracticable. This is true, but among all the social blueprints brought to reality on these shores, among the Pennsylvanias and Georgias and Brook Farms, the Dedham experiment stands out by virtue of its relative endurance. In the long history of American utopias, any which lasted the better part of fifty years must be accounted a success.

II

A Provincial Town, 1686–1736

At the end of its first fifty years Dedham was still a static rural village. A hundred and fifty years later it was to be a county seat, a thriving commercial and manufacturing center just beginning to merge into the industrial belt forming around Boston, and a town which had long been a focus for the vigorous political activity popularly associated with the Jacksonian era. How did Dedham pass from the one scene to the other? The beginnings of the transition can be seen in the story of the next fifty years of the town's existence. It is a peculiar, frustrating story, for the continuities of the period nearly balanced the changes, while the changes themselves were often elusively evolutionary. Yet it is a story well worth following, for out of the intricate flux of events emerges the certainty that the village community had physically disintegrated, the probability that a society more accustomed to social diversity and political dissent had begun to evolve, and the possibility that the way had been prepared for the gospel of individual rights which would be preached during the American Revolution and widely practiced in the nineteenth-century nation.

6

Toward a New Community[1]

〰〰〰〰〰〰〰〰〰〰〰〰〰〰〰〰〰〰〰〰〰〰〰〰〰〰〰〰

NO LONGER a utopian commune, Dedham was still a community, still a small village with extensive local powers and a tattered but enduring tradition of consensus. Though the community of 1686 was less perfectly united than that of 1636, it was nonetheless the direct heir of its predecessor and any of the first signers of the Covenant would have found its atmosphere congenial. But in the next fifty years Dedham was to so fragment and finally crumble under the pressure of unprecedented growth that in the end it could hardly be said that much of the reality of community remained. In its place would come a new and more complex definition of community which, if less satisfactory than the old, was at least better suited to the changing times.

* * *

An acute observer could have seen the problem coming long before it reached a crisis. The trouble was really very straightforward, nothing as subtle as the lightly shifting circum-

1. This chapter is indebted to "The Transformation of Dedham, Massachusetts, 1715–1750," by Edward M. Cook, Jr., an undergraduate honors thesis for Harvard University completed in 1965. Mr. Cook and the author conducted their research into the history of eighteenth-century Dedham simultaneously, constantly exchanging ideas and advice, and ultimately reaching a large measure of agreement in their analyses of the events at hand. Mr. Cook is extending his analysis of the town into the later eighteenth century.

stances and spiritual entropy which had brought a modicum
of change to the previous era. The town had begun with several
score families huddled together in a village in one corner of
a tract 200 miles square. Centrifugal forces—the sustained
growth of the population, the granting of ever more distant
dividends of land, the slow consolidation of individual holdings
around these grants—had tugged at the village almost from
the moment of its creation. By 1686 a number of farms had
finally coalesced around outlying holdings, barns were being
moved out to these sites, and the forces pulling their owners
away from the village had grown quite intense. One by one
these farmers began to decide to end their long daily treks
between village and barn by building homes out on their farms
and abandoning their residences in the village. As the process
of consolidation of farms continued and the population rose
from over 600 in 1686 on toward 1,200 in 1736, the number
of such decisions multiplied. A multitude of these individual
actions posed fundamental questions which would demand an
answer before the town had passed through its second half-
century: What would happen when groups of these men, and
their sons as they in turn made farms on still more distant
grants of land, found the focus of their lives removed from the
old village—perhaps so far removed that they no longer felt
themselves a part of its consensus and began to seek churches
and communities of their own? At what point would these
tendencies threaten the integrity of the community? What would
be the response of the community to this threat?

Yet it took a long time for the problem to come to a head.
Only after 1720 did the town confront directly all the issues
raised by the dispersal of the population, largely because
dispersal had little apparent effect on the community until this
time. To be sure, by 1720 four new towns had been carved
out of the old Dedham grant, but three of these resulted from the
movement of population into very remote parts of the town-

ship, and their great distance from Dedham village made their separation relatively painless.[2]

The first two towns to split off had actually been sponsored by Dedham, partially out of an urge to create buffer settlements between the village and the Indian-infested wilderness. Medfield was settled in 1649 by a select group of Dedham inhabitants. It was situated in virgin territory more than ten miles southeast of the village. Wrentham was begun thirteen years later, when a group of "persons as are [judged] fit to carry on such a work in church and commonwealth" [3] were permitted to settle in another corner of the grant over twenty miles to the south. Incorporated as independent towns in 1651 and 1673, respectively, Medfield and Wrentham served admirably the function for which they were intended, each absorbing in the course of the seventeenth century at least one devastating Indian raid which would otherwise have struck Dedham. These early and obviously functional secessions did not occur without difficulties; quarrels over the responsibility for public debts and over land rights marred the separation of Medfield, while the Wrentham settlers grew so exasperated at Dedham's reluctance to grant them independence that they accused the mother-town of keeping them in colonial dependency.[4] There is, however,

2. The pertinent information can be found in *Records,* III–VI, through the indexes under "Bogastow" or "Medfield" (1648–1653), "Wolomonapog" or "Wrentham" (1660–1675), "Needham" (1705–1713), and "Bellingham" (1701–1721). For brief accounts of each case see Mann, *Historical Annals of Dedham, Massachusetts . . .* (Dedham, 1847), 1–26, 97–103; Frank Smith, *A History of Dedham, Massachusetts* (Dedham, Mass., 1936), 6, 383. George K. Clarke, *History of Needham, Massachusetts* (Cambridge, Mass., 1912) is typical of the antiquarian local histories which exist for each of the towns in question and offer further details. The secession of Needham and that of Walpole (1721–1724) will be discussed at a later point in the chapter. See chapters 7 and 8 for details of the town's political and social structure in these years, including population figures.

3. *Records,* IV, 43.

4. Massachusetts Historical Society, *Photostats,* October 15, 1673.

no evidence that Dedham village saw the secession of either
Medfield or Wrentham as a threat to its integrity.

The secession of Bellingham in 1719 fell into a somewhat
similar pattern. The area was a little west of faraway Wrentham and was cursed with an abundance of hills and a scarcity
of good soil. Its inhabitants were a mixed lot of subsistence
farmers. Some of them were Quakers and Baptists from neighboring Rhode Island, men who wanted to conduct their simple
affairs in peace and obscurity. Since the inhabitants had purchased or inherited the lots into which the Dedham proprietors
had divided the area, there were no issues of disputed title to
lead Dedham to obstruct the process of separation. On May
11, 1719:

> The inhabitants of this town [living] in that tract of land lying
> between Mendon and Wrentham presented a petition to this town
> praying that they may be set off from this town in order to [become]
> a township. The town has granted it, provided . . . [the petitioners]
> can unite and incorporate together . . . [successfully, so] as to
> capacitate them to manage the affairs of a town and have the [neces-
> sary] approbation of the General Court.[5]

All was done as Dedham ordered and in the same year Bellingham became an independent town without muss, fuss, or
bother.

Neither these separations nor the general growth of population which lay behind them had provoked a crisis of identity.
The increase of the population *had* helped bring about the loss
of some peripheral lands and, inside the village itself, *had*
played some role in the decline of the overt utopian impulse.
That increase was continuing. But within its large circle of
remaining lands the village continued in relative harmony
through the end of the seventeenth century and into the first
decades of the eighteenth. There were even hints of the rebirth
of the utopian policies of the previous generation. The Reverend

5. *Records*, VI, 187.

Belcher's attempt to rely upon private contributions made some headway and for a time it began to seem that a sense of voluntary responsibility for the support of religion could be restored. The ancient corporate restriction on the alienation of land to strangers was temporarily revived.[6] Still going its way largely free of interference by the higher authorities of the colony, Dedham was entering the new century in many ways as autonomous and cohesive a community as ever.

Or so it might have seemed to a traveler hastily gobbling his dinner at Fisher's Tavern on his way through Dedham along the highway from Boston to New York. But men who lived in the town no doubt knew better. The consequences of growth were not so easily escaped. Already, beneath the superficial unity of the thirty-odd years after 1686, growth, dispersion, and diversity had begun to split the Dedham community into distinct and increasingly antagonistic sections. Within a short distance of the original village were emerging no less than five *ad hoc* societies, each of which was shortly to insist on its independence. Half-hidden at first, soon their grievances would threaten to bring about what some men feared would be the total destruction of Dedham.[7]

As they evolved in the years after 1686, the various sections of the town fell geographically into two adjoining tiers of three, each tier aligned along a north-south axis. Five to ten miles northwest of the old village was a cluster of farmhouses which had begun to form after King Philip's War and which contained several hundred persons by the turn of the century. In 1711 this area was to gain incorporation as the town of Needham.[8] Late in the seventeenth century another hamlet had arisen around the town sawmill some twelve miles south-

6. *Records,* V, 294.
7. The descriptions of the evolving "sections" are largely and of necessity from sources covering the years 1725–1750, the assumption being that some characteristics evident in 1725–1750 (after the crisis) must have had their origins in the years 1710–1725.
8. Again, see G. K. Clarke, *History of Needham, Massachusetts.*

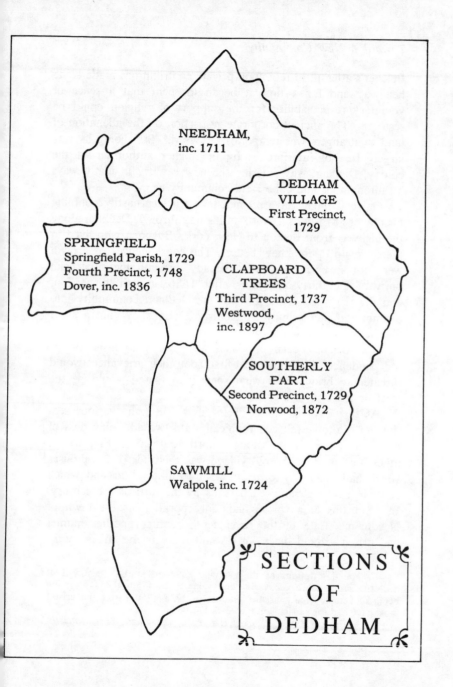

NEEDHAM,
inc. 1711

DEDHAM
VILLAGE
First Precinct,
1729

SPRINGFIELD
Springfield Parish, 1729
Fourth Precinct, 1748
Dover, inc. 1836

CLAPBOARD
TREES
Third Precinct, 1737
Westwood,
inc. 1897

SOUTHERLY
PART
Second Precinct, 1729
Norwood, 1872

SAWMILL
Walpole, inc. 1724

SECTIONS
OF
DEDHAM

west of Dedham. After 1705 the Dedham proprietors' division and sale of the land in this region hastened settlement, and in 1724 the "sawmill" inhabitants incorporated as the town of Walpole.[9] Situated between Needham and Walpole was the straggling collection of farmsteads known as "Springfield." This area emerged from the coming turmoil as the Fourth Precinct of Dedham, but had to wait until 1836 for final incorporation as the town of Dover.[10]

To the east, nestled alongside and slightly inside the sweeping arc formed by Needham, Springfield, and Walpole, lay a second triad. Down beside Walpole was an area known only as "the southerly part of town." In the course of the events to follow this would become the Second Precinct and, in 1872, the town of Norwood.[11] Directly north of the Southerly or Second Precinct was the middle component of the second triad, "Clapboard Trees." Only three miles from the Dedham meeting-house, "Clapboard Trees" eventually became the Third Precinct, though not until 1897 was it incorporated as Westwood, Massachusetts.[12] The third and uppermost component of the eastern tier was Dedham village itself, naturally known as the First Precinct when the time came for such mechanical nomenclature.

Walpole, Springfield, and Needham—southerly part, Clapboard Trees and Dedham village—the terms were many and perhaps confusing, but the message they spelled out could not have been more clear. The slow dispersal of the second and third generations of Dedham families was finally clouding the definition of "community." The village had been quite ready to let remote Medfield, Wrentham, and later Bellingham go

9. See Willard De Lue, *The Story of Walpole* (Norwood, Mass., 1925).
10. See Frank Smith, *History of Dover* (Boston, Mass., 1896). Tax lists included in *Records,* VI and in the manuscript records at the Dedham Town Hall will confirm the relative poverty of the area.
11. See Frank Smith, *A History of Dedham,* 104–7, 383.
12. See George Willis Cooke, *A History of the Clapboard Trees or Third Parish* (Boston, Mass., 1887).

their separate ways. Yet it never occurred to the leaders of
the village that "Dedham" was to mean only the small area
encompassing the original settlement and meetinghouse. Surely
the sons who had moved a mere three or five or even ten
miles away were still a part of the community? But the sons
had begun to have different ideas.

The grievances of the sections were often no more than
the grievances of dispersion, the classic grievances of groups
of New England farmers who lived a long hard journey away
from the church, the meetinghouse, and the school of their native
township. The themes that recurred in hundreds of petitions to
town meetings and legislative assemblies all over New England
were the themes that were to characterize the sectional struggle
in Dedham. And they were usually legitimate themes. The
areas which became Needham and Walpole and the Springfield
area as well were certainly too far from the old village center,
while the "southerly part" had at best marginal access to the
common institutions of the town. It was not fair that a man
who sought the word of God or small justice should have to
walk five miles or more over miserable roads in order to obtain
either. Nor was it fair to expect his young sons to spend hours
of each day on their way to and from the town schoolhouse.
An isolated farmer had little choice, of course, unless he lived
near the center of a neighboring town and the home town would
free him to attend worship and allow his children to attend
school there. But as isolated farmers acquired neighbors they
began to ask why they and their neighbors should not have
license to support their own institutions. Once the question had
been posed, common sense dictated a petition to the mother
town and the negative reaction of the mother town often dictated a political struggle. This was the story in Dedham.[13]

Yet Dedham also contained a major variation on this classic

13. Again, the details and results of the struggle are discussed
later and the specific sources will be cited at that point.

theme, for some of the sections' deeper grievances were really the grievances of diversity. What led at least one of Dedham's sections to petition for redress was not simply a sense of being distant but a sense of being different. Clapboard Trees, for example, was within easy walking distance of the meetinghouse. Its pleas of inconvenience had a hollow ring. But the leaders of Clapboard Trees were a wealthy, sophisticated lot, familiar with the bigwigs of provincial politics and prone to the religious liberalism that was à la mode in Boston.[14] It was only natural that they would grow tired of living in the political shadow of parochial Calvinist leaders from the populous and therefore politically dominant center of town. As for the other sections, the men of the sawmill hamlet were so insistent on forming their own church that they, too, may have been using the excuse of distance (legitimate in their case) to hide their craving for a different emphasis in religion. And the relative youth of the inhabitants of all the other sections no doubt played some role in giving them a sense of uniqueness and an eagerness to free themselves from the old village elite. (Their relative lack of wealth probably did not add to their resentments, for it was as yet very slight. And in any event the poorest of all the sections, Springfield, ended up allied with the village!)

This explains why all the sections ultimately sought not merely convenient institutions but complete independence. There were many possible accommodations short of full secession. Men from an outlying area could seek permission to pay their taxes to and make use of the institutions of neighboring towns. Or they could ask to be allowed to hire their own minister, thereby becoming a distinct "Parish." An added adjustment on this level would be a plea for the hiring of a second schoolmaster who would peripatate the town's periphery from one outlying group of pupils to another. Just short of

14. Cook, "Transformation of Dedham," includes a fine analysis of the nature and motives of the men of Clapboard Trees. See p. 62, for example.

independence was the status of "Precinct," a status recognized by colony law. A Precinct usually provided the peripheral group its own church, school, tax assessors, and militia officers, preserving the unity of the town only insofar as all Precincts operated under a common town board of selectmen and sent a single town representative to the General Court. Though all Dedham's sections began by petitioning for such lesser favors, all but one quickly passed on to a demand for recognition as independent townships.[15] The men of the sections soon realized that they wanted more than access to institutions and more even than their own particular churches, branch schools, and minor officers. They wanted what only total independence would recognize, the right to shape their own communities. Only in this way would the sense of communal uniqueness which had evolved in each find its fullest expression. Mere personal ambition may have moved the leaders of this or that section to push on toward complete independence, for with independence they would be able to build political careers as the selectmen and representatives of their new township. But it was a deeper sense of communal identity and broader desire for communal self-determination among the people of each section that made these men leaders and which supported them in their attempts to by-pass interim concessions and obtain independence.

In this light the dilemma posed by the emergence of sections in Dedham takes on a universal form. The problem of maintaining a sense of community in the face of dispersion and diversity has been faced by traditional communities countless times in the past and is still being faced in the rural societies of our time. And the solution offered by the dissatisfied components of the overgrown society is always the same and always conservative: Reduce the old community to a set of

15. See the following discussion for specific data. Springfield is the exception.

entirely new communities each of which will be small and cohesive enough to regain the sense of unity. Whether in the
towns of old New England or in the peasant villages of modern
Spain, the communal impulse is strong and enduring. Growth
does not erase it entirely, but only forces it into expressing
itself on a different level.[16]

* * *

From the beginning of the ensuing struggle the leaders of
the village resisted the growing demands of the sections. They
resisted because these demands threatened to weaken the extended community which had grown up over the years and
which was still under their political control.[17] They vigorously
opposed the demands for secession which ultimately developed,
maintaining that "greater Dedham" was still a viable community.
The sections fought back and the struggle culminated in a
political battle for control of the town, a battle which itself
ended in violence. But the tale is more than the tale of the
collision of two definitions of community. The effects of the
battle were far-reaching and its outcome was a third and
strikingly novel definition.

Open sparring had begun as early as 1704. For several
years previously the town's tax-assessment lists had been
divided into two parts corresponding roughly to the embryonic
divisions in the distribution of the population.[18] The first part

16. Susan Tax Freeman, "Religious Aspects of the Social Organization of a Castilian Village," 34–37.
17. The yearly tax lists and records of elections in *Records* V, VI
reveal that the selectmen's offices were the almost exclusive property
of men living in the old village center. Even after the population of
the outlying areas matched that of the village, this was slow to change,
since the very distance voters from these areas had to travel made it
difficult for them to muster their forces at the meetinghouse. See also
Footnote 22.
18. *Records*, V, 232ff., and VI, tax lists following 1730. Because
of the contemporary transition in methods of dating the new year,

of each list included mostly men from the "East End," as the old center of town was then known. The other part included many men living in the far southwestern end of the old village, further southwest in Clapboard Trees, and in other outlying areas. Until 1704, virtually all of the town's selectmen had been men on the first half of the list, men from the old village. The election of that year changed things abruptly. Three of the five incumbent selectmen, Samuel Guild, Joshua Fisher, and Joseph Fairbanks, were turned out of office even though all were experienced leaders. The one thing the three had in common besides their experience was the fact that all lived in the area included in the first half of the tax list. In their places the meeting of March 6, 1704, installed Ashael Smith, Amos Fisher, and Nathaniel Gay. Among themselves these men could muster just one year's previous experience in the office but at least two of them, Gay and Fisher, lived in the areas included in the second half of the tax list. One of the two incumbents who were allowed to continue in office was from the same part of the list, so the net effect of the election was to place men from the outlying areas in at least a three to two majority on the board of selectmen. And since by the evidence of his very election the third new selectman, villager Ashael Smith, was probably in sympathy with this majority, the tally may well have been four to one in favor of the rebels, leaving in opposition only the one incumbent loyal to the center of town. In case the point was not clear, old Samuel Guild was also deposed as town Treasurer and was replaced by the upstart Nathaniel Gay. The victors had taken into their hands the purse strings as well as the reins of executive authority.

Whereupon there was a great to-do and all manner of complaining that the election of March 6 had been illegal because the required warning had not been given far enough in

---

the *Records* list January, February, and most March dates as falling under both the new and old years. These double dates have been modernized, March 1703–1704 becoming simply March, 1704, etc.

advance of the meeting. The old board of selectmen took it upon itself to invalidate the election at which three of their number had been ousted and to call a new election for March 27. On that day Samuel Guild was in fact re-elected selectman for the year ensuing and returned as well to the post of Treasurer, but the village incumbents Fisher and Fairbanks were again rejected and again the meeting filled their vacancies with men from the other part of town. The rebels thereby retained a bare majority on the board, and this drove a number of men from the center of town to argue before the Suffolk County Court that *both* of the March elections were invalid. The Court patiently instructed the town to call yet another election and on April 17, 1704, the rebels once again prevailed, electing the same set of men chosen at the first election on March 6! This time they made it stick.[19] Only gradually over the next several years did the center of town reassert its political control.

Though the aims of the insurgents were not made explicit at the time, it is clear that the battle which would eventually paralyze the town had its beginnings in this cloudy electoral crisis. It can hardly be an accident that the years immediately following the elections of 1704 were marked by disagreement as to whether or not every man had a compelling legal obligation to pay his share of the minister's salary. The negative position on this issue was adopted by men from the outlying areas, men who were not always eager to support a minister whom they regarded as the creature of a village establishment which cared little for their needs. A prolonged dispute over the location of highways to the southwestern part of town also flared up in these years, an issue which obviously affected men

19. *Records,* V, 318–22, 334, 341, 354, and Massachusetts Historical Society manuscripts, *Miscellaneous Bound,* April 2, 1704. The *Records* and the Massachusetts Historical Society manuscript are somewhat in contradiction regarding the import of the April complaint(s) to the County Court.

living in this peripheral area. The upstart selectman Nathaniel Gay and other men of the outlying areas precipitated these subsequent disagreements over sectional issues, and, seen in this light, their electoral victories of 1704 had probably marked the start of a general campaign against the political hegemony of the village.[20] Because they gradually lost control of the board of selectmen, and perhaps because they never really kept control of the town meeting after the disputed elections, nothing came of their efforts; but almost twenty years later a similar alliance would precipitate a far greater crisis over quite similar issues, again seeking to control the mechanisms of town government and this time seeking to force the town to grant independence to several of the outlying sections.

Whatever the exact links with the future, in 1704 the town had for the first time encountered a political crisis which stemmed from sectional jealousies. For the first time the newer parts of town had forged an electoral coalition and at least temporarily persuaded enough sympathizers to attend the meeting to ensure victory. The time had come to begin to speak of who would be the cabbages and who the kings of Dedham's political world.

Events of the following years brought the problem closer to definition. In 1710, forty of "the inhabitants of the North part of town" suddenly petitioned the General Court for permission to incorporate as a town. The petitioners cited the usual problems of distance and inconvenience and, brushing aside all halfway measures, offered a set of "reasons why we desire to be a township rather than a precinct." One of the

20. See *Records*, V, 353 and index under "Nathaniel Gay"; and a manuscript in the Dedham Historical Society, dated 1713, which discusses the settlement of the "ways" issue. The Gay "alliance" included a number of men who ended up legally within the First Precinct, but who lived slightly south and west of the heart of the village and who consistently placed themselves alongside the sectional dissidents of Clapboard Trees, probably for religious as well as sectional reasons.

reasons was quite revealing of the tensions developing within the town. The petitioners feared that, as a mere precinct, they would still be "under the wing" of Dedham and thus subject to "hard measures" from that town in retaliation for their bid for independence. The ultimate reason behind the request for complete independence was, however, simply that the petitioners "might be a free people of themselves." Dedham asked the General Court to delay hearings on the issue until the next year, so not until May of 1711 was the town required to "show cause if any there be why the prayers of the petitioners . . . should not be granted." At this point Dedham declared itself willing to let the secession go through but proposed a boundary line which would have sharply reduced the area of the township specified in the original petition. The General Court flatly rejected this proposal and in the same year approved the incorporation of the town of Needham.[21] Needham, the first secession since Wrentham nearly forty years before, was the first area within ten miles of the village to seek its independence. Several of its founders had been among the rebels of 1704. Their success could hardly have escaped the notice of the inhabitants of the other outlying areas of the town. Dedham's resistance was mild, but was itself a sign that the old leaders from the village were already reluctant to face the progressive falling away of the surrounding lands and inhabitants.

A set of concessions won in 1717 testified to mounting pressure from the remaining outlying areas. For the first time in years the meeting chose as Moderator (chairman) of the March election meeting a man from one of the peripheral settlements. Though the voters then returned to office two incumbent selectmen from the center of town, they also reelected incumbent Joseph Ellis, the same man they had just chosen Moderator and a resident of "the southerly part of town." And

21. Clarke, *History of Needham,* 68–76; and *Records,* VI, 60, 78, 87, 88.

they replaced the other two incumbents, men from the center of town, with two rather ambiguous novices, Nathaniel Kingsbury and William Bullard. Both of these men seem to have lived in the area that became the First Precinct, but both had namesake sons living in other parts of town and they were evidently sympathetic to the needs of those areas. For, led by the new Moderator and altered board, the town promptly voted to excuse from the minister's tax any persons living more than five miles from the meetinghouse who found it convenient to transfer their attendance and support to the church of another town. This amounted to an official admission that some members of the Dedham community would have the right to shift their religious loyalties away from the local church. It was the first general concession ever made to the needs of the outlying areas. More new ground was broken when the same meeting voted in favor of a moving school whose master would teach for several months in each of several parts of town, thereby alleviating the isolation of the sections from the old village school.[22] But because of the rising resentment of the sections these initial concessions were soon outdated.

The years of vague skirmishing drew to a close and a decade of acute political conflict was precipitated in May of 1721, when the men down at the sawmill hamlet replied to Dedham's refusal to let them hire their own minister by demanding complete independence.[23] Shortly thereafter the in-

22. See *Records,* VI, 152, 162–63, 172–73. A man's residence can usually be determined by a look at the post-1730 tax lists in *Records,* VI, and among the Town Hall manuscripts, since these lists are divided into clearly marked sectional sublists. (Where unable to establish residence from this source, the author has found Cook, "Transformation," Appendix B, useful.)

23. *Records,* VI, 206–7. The author differs somewhat from Cook in his description of the acute phases of the conflict which took place in the years 1704–1747, and likewise differs slightly in his over-all point of view. But Cook's presentation of the events following 1721 is more complete and is generally quite accurate.

habitants of Clapboard Trees together with some of those living in the southerly part of town petitioned the town "to have the meetinghouse removed [closer to their homes] or to be set off as a township or precinct." At the same time the remaining inhabitants of the southerly area petitioned "desiring the town to set them off as a township or precinct." [24] The entire area south of the village, including what became the town of Walpole, the Second Precinct and the Third Precinct, had now raised the issue of independence.

The town reacted slowly to the petition from the sawmill area, but by May of 1724 local approval had been won. Shortly thereafter the General Court gave its necessary sanction to the new township of Walpole. It is likely that the Walpole secession was pushed through the meeting by an alliance of the three petitioning areas against the center of town. And it is certain that in the very same years men from these areas allied in a vain effort to obstruct the town's decision to hire the Reverend Samuel Dexter in the place of the recently deceased Joseph Belcher. Though some of these men mixed a genuine opposition to Dexter's theology with their sectional prejudices, the chief point of the obstructionists was not narrowly theological. Their aim was to assert in yet another way the combined opposition of the peripheral areas to the continuing control of town policy by the village, and perhaps to nag the village into granting them independence.[25]

Nonetheless, after the success of the Walpole petitioners the center of town regained full control of the government. The Reverend Dexter was hired in spite of all opposition. The petition from the mixed Clapboard Trees—southerly group gathered dust over the next two years, as did the petition from the rest of the inhabitants of the southerly part of town. In

24. *Records,* VI, 219.
25. *Records,* VI, 240, 243. See Cook, "Transformation," 44, for an account of the opposition to Dexter.

a way the triple alliance of 1721–1724 had been too successful,
for in obtaining the secession of Walpole it had cost itself a
third of its voting strength!

After the separation of Walpole the potential voting power
of the remaining sections was almost exactly that of the center
of town. The sections usually held an edge over the village in
terms of total numbers of taxpayers, and after 1735 that edge
slowly increased. But until that time the edge was very slight
and, since the average taxpayer of the combined sections was
a little less wealthy than his counterpart in the village, it is
possible that a smaller percentage of the taxpayers of the
sections held enough property to qualify as voters under the
provincial law. The hovering balance of political power was
usually tipped against the leaders of the sections by two circumstances. In order for them to win control of the town meeting,
dozens of men had to be persuaded to make the tedious trip
from their distant homes to the meetinghouse. With this
miracle accomplished, the sections had achieved at best a voting
bloc equal in numbers to that of the "establishment." Final
victory depended on close cooperation between the sections
and on their winning and holding a few votes from the ranks
of the establishment.[26]

Still, time was on the side of the challengers. Every year
the absolute numbers of men within each section increased,
strengthening the developing sense of community, supporting
the argument that each section was capable of maintaining its
own church, school, and town government without financial
strain, and increasing the ambitions of the sectional leaders.
The years immediately following the secession of Walpole were
marked by a dramatic rise in the numbers of young men coming
of age.[27] To the leaders of the sections these young men who

26. Again, tax lists in *Records,* VI, give the necessary data. (See
also Cook, "Transformation," Appendices A and G.)
27. See Lockridge, "The Population of Dedham, Massachusetts,"

had grown up in an intensifying atmosphere of sectional self-consciousness were ideal political material.

What followed is in part obscure, but the result was unquestionably a complete paralysis of the mechanisms of town government. Tension built up through 1725 and 1726 as control of the town remained firmly with the village. The petition of the Clapboard Trees—southerly group was still pending. In 1726 the rest of the inhabitants of the southerly part of town submitted a modified petition, this time unequivocally asking for complete independence and this time addressing themselves directly to the General Court.[28] Such was the state of affairs as of the election meeting of March 6, 1727. The election was so hotly contested that the meeting took two days to complete its work. The selectmen's posts were opened to nominations one by one, instead of all together as was the custom. Once the candidates for each vacancy were known, a secret, written ballot was held. For the first time since 1690 every single incumbent was thrown out of office. In their places the voters put three men from Clapboard Trees and two men from the center of town who were evidently sympathetic to the demands of the rebels.[29]

As might be expected, the meeting whose majority had thrown the establishment out of office went on to consider the two pending petitions for separation. But the tide had reached its high point and could go no further. The leaders of the establishment must have realized that men from Clapboard Trees and probably from other sections as well had conspired to turn out en masse and seize control of the meeting. They no doubt responded by rounding up enough of the

---

331, 341–43; the surge of births in the years around 1700 was the cause of the surge of maturations after 1724.

28. *Journal of the House of Representatives of Massachusetts Bay* (Boston, Mass., 1919–1965), VI, 15, 51, 141, 153, 173. The later episodes of this latter petition will be treated in the following discussion.

29. *Records*, VI, 270ff.

lazy yeomen of the village to restore their majority. When the meeting ended the petitions for separation had not been approved and the rebels had to settle for control of the board of selectmen. At subsequent meetings in May and July every attempt to ease the lot of the two petitioning areas was rejected.[30]

In November the struggle swayed back in favor of the rebels, who managed to elect Joseph Ellis the town's representative to the General Court and to have his election certified by the Court despite the complaint of forty-nine men from the village that the whole process had been illegal. Though Ellis turned out to be no mere errand-boy for the rebels (he was in fact re-elected through the next six years regardless of which party controlled the town), it was no small advantage to the petitioning areas that the town was now represented in the colony's highest counsels by a man who knew their side of the story. And their initial victory in electing Ellis against strong establishment opposition encouraged them to continue their efforts to win complete control of the town and thereby force it to approve their secession.[31] But the cost of victory had been high, as the Reverend Samuel Dexter sadly observed in his diary:

[There] was a general meeting of our people for the choice of a representative, and a very uncomfortable one it was. The people, or at least many of them, discovered great spirit and party zeal, and there was great jars and contentions and animosity among them and broke up their meeting. [They] appointed a second and still continued their noise and confusion and have, I fear, laid the foundation of a very bitter contention.[32]

The next town meeting was the scheduled election of local officers in March, 1728. The rebels were evidently afraid that

30. *Records,* VI, 273–74.
31. *Records,* VI, 274; Cook, "Transformation," 48, which cites in turn *Journal of the House of Representatives of Massachusetts,* VIII, 5, 14.
32. Dexter diary, (in manuscript in the Dedham Historical Society,) entry following October 29, 1727.

their narrow and unstable majority could not be held together through another prolonged electoral contest, much less long enough to push through the pending petitions for separation, for they rushed through a resolution that "the town would go on with this present meeting . . . only exempting such from voting that were rated only for their poll." [33] This amounted to a declaration that, contrary to province law, a man with any taxable property at all could vote in the meeting. Since the outlying areas were in general a little less well off than the village and therefore proportionately more of their male inhabitants did not hold enough property to qualify as voters, this opening of the gates to men who held so much as a penny-worth of property was bound to increase the rebels' majority.

Thus armed by illegality they proceeded toward the election of another board of selectmen loyal to their cause. John Gay, Comfort Starr, Joseph Smith—three of the party stalwarts— were re-elected by the now-customary secret ballot. Then suddenly the meeting broke off without so much as a decision to adjourn. As the courts of the colony subsequently determined:

> John Gay, tailor, Benjamin Gay, and Joseph Smith with force of arms did then and there disturb the said meeting . . . and did willfully interrupt and stop the business of the day, unlawfully commanding Ebenezer Woodward, who was at said meeting legally chosen Moderator, to be silent and depart the said assembly. . . . And the said John Gay with force as aforesaid did then and there assault and strike the said Ebenezer Woodward in the actual discharge of his duty. . . . And other enormities the said John and Benjamin Gay and Joseph Smith did there commit.[34]

No doubt bothered by the illegal voting standards forced on the meeting by the rebels, standards for which he as Moderator could be held responsible under the law, Woodward had

33. *Records,* VI, 281–82, contain the full record of this meeting. See the next chapter for a discussion of the suffrage requirements.
34. Under "John Gay" in the manuscript records of the General Sessions of the Peace for 1728, in the office of the Clerk of the Superior Court of Suffolk County, Boston.

probably expressed his doubts or even tried to adjourn the
meeting. Infuriated by his interference, three of the rebels had
stepped up with muskets in hand and ordered Woodward to
leave. When he refused they struck him and the meeting dissolved in chaos. The marvelous political machinery of the New
England Town had been reduced to a brawl.

The town reassembled next day and elected the rest of the
rebel slate under the same illegal suffrage requirement. But the
damage had been done. The three rowdies were taken to court,
found guilty of disrupting the meeting, and heavily fined.
Though the protests of the village party against the election did
not lead the General Court to disqualify the outlaw selectmen,
enough moderate voters had been sufficiently shocked to swing
the weight of town opinion back against the rebel cause. All
efforts to approve the secession of the petitioning sections were
rejected out of hand. The village party began a legal vendetta
against Nathaniel Gay for imagined flaws in his accounts as
constable back in 1724. And the election of the following year
showed that the village could forge its own political alliances.
The meeting removed all five rebel selectmen and elected in
their places four village men and one man from the "Springfield" area. Immediately thereafter the town made Springfield
a Precinct.[35] The swap was obvious: in exchange for shifting
their votes to the side of the establishment the Springfield men
won the semi-autonomous status of a Precinct and one seat on
the new board of selectmen. To add insult to injury, the
alliance had pointedly elected the much-abused Ebenezer Woodward to one of the selectmen's posts!

The adversaries might have continued thus at one another's
throats forever, but by 1729 it was clear to the higher authorities of Massachusetts that no final decision could be expected
from the town meeting. The struggle had shifted back and
forth for years, marked by steadily deepening animosities and
by a swelling flood of petitions and counter-petitions to the

35. *Records,* VI, 282ff., 298; Cook, "Transformation," 51.

General Court. The Court certified the political bankruptcy of the town when it sent a special committee to Dedham to seek a compromise. On hearing the report of its committee the Court imposed a settlement, denying all petitions for independence, creating a single new Precinct out of all the southerly part of town together with the Clapboard Trees, and voiding Dedham's unilateral grant of a Precinct to Springfield. After a last spasm of debate within the deadlocked town, the decision was implemented. The town thenceforth labeled the old village the First Precinct, the secessionist areas the Second or Southerly Precinct, and the remaining part of town the Springfield Parish.[36]

There was a little more sorting out yet to be done. The Clapboard Trees faction was not content to be lumped with the rest of the Second Precinct, nor were they satisfied when the General Court tried to put an end to their pestering by moving them back as part of the First Precinct in 1734. The liberal religious views of some of their leaders had found no sympathy in the churches of either Precinct. In 1735 these leaders joined with other religious malcontents from an adjoining part of the First Precinct and on their own dubious authority hired a minister whose theology was more congenial. This led to renewed quarreling in the town meeting. The quarreling led in turn, as the Clapboard Trees group had no doubt expected, to a renewed interposition by a General Court anxious to clean up the mess in Dedham. By the beginning of 1737 the skilled troublemakers from Clapboard Trees had won recognition as a Third Precinct.[37]

When in 1748 the General Court at last granted obscure Springfield Parish the status of a Fourth Precinct, the arrangement which was to characterize the town through most of the next century was complete. Exhausted by more than twenty-

---

36. Cook, "Transformation," 52; *Records,* VI, 300–20; *Journals of the House of Representatives,* X, 168, 193; XI, 197, 227, 230, 240, 331, 342; XII, 44, 68, 120, 161. The present account is somewhat simplified.

37. George W. Cooke, *A History of the Clapboard Trees,* 11–25.

five years of conflict, the town accepted the quadripartite divisions imposed by the General Court. Further internicine struggles were averted by means of a system of proportional representation which evolved in the 1730's and 1740's. In its final form this system tacitly allotted one selectman's post to each section or special interest group within the town: one to the First Precinct, one to those First Precinct inhabitants who attended the Third Precinct church, and one each to the Second, Third, and Fourth Precincts.[38] Neither side's definition of community had won and neither would ever win. The battle had ended in a cease-fire, an armistice, a truce.

* * *

Seen from the point of view of the past, the events of the early eighteenth century were a disaster. Weakened by the dispersal of Dedham society, the communal impulse had sought rebirth in the creation of a set of smaller communities. But the effort had only led to internal conflict and ultimately to a political truce which sanctioned the fragmentation of human loyalties. Paradoxically, the half-victory of the outlying areas was in many respects more damaging to the ideal of community than were the assorted grievances which had led them into the struggle in the first place. Now every man was *in the eyes of the law* two men, owing allegiance to a Precinct as well as to the town. It could be even worse: a man represented in the General Court because he was a citizen of Dedham might actually live in the First Precinct, pay his taxes and serve in the militia platoon there, yet be represented on the Dedham board of selectmen by virtue of his identity as one of those First Precinct inhabitants who attended church in the Third Precinct! Where were his loyalties? Where was his community?

38. Frank Smith, *History of Dover,* 26–28; Cook, "Transformation," 71.

The communal impulse was by no means dead. It still existed within each Precinct and after a century or more each Precinct would become an independent town. But for a long time to come the sense of community would have to exist in an uneasy tension with the institutionalized diversity that was the product of the struggle. The men of each Precinct would still live insofar as it lay within their power the lives of members of an autonomous and cohesive community, yet it would not be entirely within their power to live such lives. Members of a Precinct, they were also members of the larger township; and they would remain both, because a revival of the battle for complete separation would only bring renewed political chaos. The outcome of their struggle for independence was an unsatisfying compromise which had so frozen the terms of existence that neither the town nor any group within it could hope to revive the blend of unity and autonomy the town as a whole had known in 1636 or even 1686.

The truce which prevailed could not even be dignified with the name of a new synthesis. It had as yet no ideology which could persuade men to embrace it as a positive good. The old way had been simple, the new was complex; the old had been unitary, the new was federal; the old had been organic, the new was mechanical; the old had been voluntary, the new was imposed. Small wonder no one cared to elevate this truce to the level of a new system of values. The residue of the old ideology of voluntary communal consensus would remain with the inhabitants of Dedham for some time to come. It would remain because it was more satisfying than no ideology at all and because the coming of the new order had not robbed it of all basis in reality.

But to look at the new order entirely from the point of view of the past is to see only the tragic side of events. The arrangement had some very practical advantages. The inexorable growth of the town had demanded that some accommodation be made between the fact of increasing diversity and the ideal of communal unity. Presented with the alternatives of an amorphous "greater Dedham" or the secession of the evolving subcommunities, the town had failed to agree on either alternative. The General Court had then imposed a compromise which had the power of law and at least restored peace to the town after years of harmful conflict. Furthermore, the men of Dedham now had both the satisfaction of belonging to the highly localized community of a Precinct and at the same time the benefits of membership in what was becoming one of the largest and most influential country towns in Massachusetts. Finally, the General Court's decisions embodied two important steps toward the legal recognition of liberty of conscience. The men of each Precinct could now establish their own church. Thus, though the religious liberals of Clapboard Trees did not win independence, they did get their own Precinct, and with that status came the right to establish a church whose minister expressed their particular convictions. The Court went on to allow individuals of a similarly liberal cast of mind who lived in other Precincts to excuse themselves from their conservative local churches and transfer their taxes and attendance to the Clapboard Trees church. The avenues of religious choice had been increased to this degree.

So the truce which had left the locus of communal loyalties unresolved had also given Dedham peace and perhaps shown the way toward a radically new experience of community, one in which diversity and unity could exist together and in which the law would protect the former from the excesses of the latter. For the moment these were only practical advantages, but one day men would extol the benefits of social and religious diversity and idealize the individual rights of choice which followed from that diversity. For the townsmen of Dedham, the fragmentation of their community in the first half of the eighteenth century was an initial step toward this view. Most important, it was a step the inhabitants of other thriving towns in New England could have been forced to make as their towns also outgrew their village origins.

7

Toward a New Politics

THE PASSAGE OF TIME brought to Dedham more than an unforeseen definition of community, it brought as well a new politics. During these same years a host of specific changes in the operation of town government altered the impact of the town as a political institution. Beyond this, the very nature of public behavior underwent a change so profound that in the end the inhabitants of Dedham had lived through an entirely new political experience.

* * *

A vigorous town meeting of the classic mold emerged in Dedham as the seventeenth century drew to a close and the eighteenth century began.[1] The original source of all local authority, the meeting had been quiescent during the utopian age, submitting to the decisions of its selectmen, rarely taking the initiative. Now it awoke and took from the selectmen the power which had always been its to claim. The decided shift in power this awakening represented did not show itself dramatically. There occurred no constitutional crises which precipitated wholesale or grudging transfers of traditional prerogatives from the

1. See "The Evolution of Massachusetts Town Government," Kenneth A. Lockridge and Alan Kreider, for a more detailed analysis of this emergence and for evidence of a parallel transition in neighboring Watertown. *Records*, III–VI, are the sources for the analysis of events in Dedham. They are cited here only where quoted or when specific cases are cited in the text.

selectmen to the meeting. On the contrary, overt conflict between the two bodies continued to be rare. It was only over a
period of thirty or forty years that a series of small innovations
in procedure testified to the rising assertiveness of the townsmen
in their public town meeting and finally left no doubt that they
had assumed the leadership of town affairs in a way unheard
of in the past.

The most apparent evidence of the accumulation of power
in the hands of the town meeting was the increase in the number
and length of public meetings. While in the decades before 1686
the men of the town had assembled on the average only twice
each year, after the turn of the century they were meeting four
or five times a year.[2] At the same time the list of problems
treated at each meeting grew longer and longer. And, though
the selectmen still called some meetings on their own initiative,
others were called by the townsmen themselves before they
adjourned from the previous meeting. In one respect these
changes were a normal result of the growth of the population.
The sheer volume of business generated by the enlarged community often forced the townsmen to end a meeting late in the
day with the agenda still unfinished. They could only wearily
vote to adjourn until a day when they could meet again to resume
consideration of the swollen agenda. But the greater frequency
and length of town meetings cannot be traced solely to communal growth, for the volume of business handled by the meeting increased much more rapidly than the population in the
critical years of the transition. The town meeting was extending
its powers by taking over a larger share of the total business, and

2. This includes the meetings by adjournment described below,
which were technically only extensions of the original meeting but
were in all except the legal sense distinct meetings. If these are not
included, the average goes up from two meetings a year before 1686
to three and one-half thereafter, still a rise of seventy-five percent.

The suffrage, that is, the actual level of voting membership in
the meeting, will be discussed later in the chapter. But there is every
indication that *all* townsmen could attend and speak to any meeting.

the records reveal that the business it was appropriating involved matters of real consequence in every sphere of governmental activity. Point by point, year after year, the meeting was adjusting the mechanisms of government so as to acquire more of the substance of power.

One of the ways the townsmen expressed their reluctance to accept the dominance of the selectmen was their use of a new local office, that of Moderator. Occasionally after 1690 and regularly after 1715 they chose one man to preside over the business of each meeting. Always a respected townsman, the Moderator was not necessarily a selectman. Whether or not one of the selectmen would be asked to direct the assembly depended solely upon the town's mood. The townsmen supplemented this innovation by gaining greater control over the list of business to be considered. The General Court had provided that the meeting must limit its debates to the items listed on an agenda prepared well in advance, and the Court had left the contents of the agenda almost entirely to the discretion of the selectmen. Under the ponderous mechanisms of the law, it took a petition signed by ten freeholders to force the selectmen to add an item of business to the agenda. With brilliant finesse, the Dedham meeting circumvented the selectmen's control by arranging that the last proposal on each agenda be "to do other business that may concern the town," an open-ended clause which left the townsmen free to consider any matters they pleased! [3]

Control of the Moderator aside, an ever larger share of the local power of appointment fell to the meeting after 1686, as the whole town created several new offices and began to fill offices formerly filled by the selectmen. Thus, the meeting took over the election of the constables and created the post of treasurer, thereby gaining control over the men who respectively collected and disbursed the town's revenues. And, while the selectmen

---

3. *Acts and Resolves . . . of the Province of Massachusetts Bay . . .* (Boston, Mass., 1869–1922), II, 30ff.; *Records,* VI, 274.

were still permitted to act as the assessors of each man's share of the tax burden, at elections the townsmen now stated that their executives were authorized to serve as assessors only "for this present year." [4] This was a reminder to the selectmen that the townsmen were looking over their shoulders as they made up the tax lists. If too many men thought that their property taxes were not fairly assessed, the delegation of power could be withdrawn from the selectmen and other men appointed in their stead at the very next election.

It was also a mark of the times that whenever new legislation was called for it was now the town meeting rather than the board of selectmen which wrote the needed ordinances. The problem here, however, was that the first selectmen had written such a comprehensive set of bylaws during the years following the founding of the town that they had virtually removed this sphere of power from future consideration. But the meeting more than made up for a lack of opportunity in the legislative sphere by moving toward close control of that essential of political power, money. No longer did the selectmen raise and spend local revenues subject only to the most casual supervision from the taxpayers. The annual public appointment of constables, assessors, and a treasurer was just one part of a system of public financial checks imposed in these years. Henceforth every tax was specifically authorized by the town: "The town by vote have granted a rate for defraying town charges." On publishing the actual list of assessments, the selectmen were careful to invoke this authorization: "This day a rate is made by virtue of an act of the town at their general meeting." Nor did the town always approve the appropriations or the revenues requested by the selectmen: "It was proposed to the town whether they would do anything towards the building of a schoolhouse in any part of the town. It was passed in the negative. Also proposed to the town whether they would grant twenty pounds for defraying

4. *Records,* VI, 28.

other charges arising in the town. It passed in the negative." [5] The system reached its peak in the establishment of a committee to audit the selectmen's expenditures. Yearly after 1726, "it was proposed to the town whether it be their mind to choose a committee to examine all the accounts between the town treasurer and the town. Voted in the affirmative." [6] The members of this committee were customarily not selectmen; they constituted an independent body responsible directly to the town. Appointed well before approval of the accounts was due, the members had ample time in which to pry and quibble to ensure that not a sixpence had been wasted.

The meeting even became entangled to an ever-increasing degree in the administrative trivia which plague every government. The right to hang a gate across a public road, adjustments in property lines, reconsiderations of tax assessments . . . for some reason many of the farmers who wanted such small favors began to take their pleas before the public assembly as often as they went to the selectmen. A subtle shift in the locus of political allegiance was taking place as these men sought and received assistance from their equals instead of from their leaders. At the same time certain of the most momentous administrative decisions, such as the expansion of the meetinghouse or the disposal of surplus revenue, were no longer left to the discretion of the selectmen.[7] That the townsmen should begin to occupy themselves with such matters implies a widespread lack of confidence in the board of selectmen.

Back in 1639, when the town had concluded that its interests were "nothing furthered" by allowing all the many problems of the community to be discussed at the general meeting, the solution had been the annual election of a board of selectmen. Now that the town meeting was again immersing itself in the details of local government the problem of administrative efficiency

5. *Records,* V, 225, 236; VI, 309.
6. *Records,* VI, 176.
7. The examples cited will be found in *Records,* V, 286; VI, 215.

posed itself anew. This time, however, the meeting could not very well relieve itself of the press of business by creating a board of selectmen, for this time there already existed such a board and the meeting was overloaded with work largely because it was unwilling to let the selectmen continue to handle the lion's share of the business! A way out of the renewed dilemma was found in the creation of a series of *ad hoc* committees. Whereas the selectmen were elected for a full year and could consider any issue, the members of the committees were restricted to a single issue and served at the town's pleasure. There were few *ad hoc* committees held before 1686, but their number increased in the ensuing decades to the point at which several would be active at once, each assigned a problem which would formerly have been left to the selectmen, and each responding closely to the wishes of the town. Through the use of this device the town came to resemble a sort of political amoeba, shooting out functional pseudopods as it chose, digesting with ease the mass of responsibilities which were the consequence of its new power.[8]

With all the increased activity went a new spirit in the town meeting. "The town voted" this, "the town ordered" that, "the town" saw fit to appoint, to authorize, to decide many matters. This phrase "the town" recurs throughout the records as if part of a secular liturgy. Moreover, the new popular spirit expressed itself in divisions between groups of townsmen as well as in their collective assertions of power. The public disagreements which, though increasing, had been exceptions before 1686 had now so increased as sometimes to seem the new rule. So the custom of decisions "by general agreement" was discarded along with the custom of passive obedience to the selectmen, and by the end of its first century Dedham had a town meeting that could match the legend: active, suspicious, contradictory, and cantankerous.

8. The increase in Dedham ran from approximately five to seventeen committees per decade. See Lockridge and Kreider, "The Evolution of Massachusetts Town Government," 574, for this and other relevant tabulations.

On the reverse of the coin was the declining influence of the board of selectmen. Weakened by the town's appropriation of various of its most useful powers, the board was further undermined by its constituents' growing independence at election time. The town more often rejected incumbent selectmen and stepped up its recruitment of new men. Together with a reduction in the number of selectmen's posts from seven to five, this made it difficult for an ambitious man to build a long career in the office.[9] (Fewer posts meant fewer opportunities to obtain election, and once elected a man was likely to be replaced within a year, perhaps by a novice; he might be returned to office after a few years, but he would be lucky if he were returned more than twice.) Soon no one could be found to match the master selectmen of the seventeenth century, men like Eleazer Lusher or Joshua Fisher, men with twenty and more terms under their broad belts. It became unusual to hear of a man who had served

9. See Table One, in this chapter.

The Decline in the Experiential Resources of the Board of Selectmen, 1639–1736.

MEASURE *	TO 1687	1687–1736
1. Percent turnover in average year.	27% (1.88 of 7)	40% (2 of 5)
2. Percent recruitment in average year.	10% (.7 of 7)	22% (1.1 of 5)
3. Total new men recruited.	35	55
4. Average number of terms served during his career by a selectman first elected in this period.	7.6	4.8
5. Percent of selectmen first elected in this period who serve more than ten terms.	35%	7%
6. Cumulative experience of the average board of selectmen, in years.	50	25

* All figures are rounded off. The last is an approximation derived indirectly from other data.

as many as ten terms. The net effect of the town's electoral innovations was to cut in half the total experience represented by the average board of selectmen. Never again would the town face, as it had in 1671, a group of men with a century of cumulative service in the office. Insofar as the board's power had rested on the experience of its members, that power was now considerably diminished.[10]

Though the board had lost many of its powers and though the selectmen had lost some of the electoral support they had once enjoyed, the office was far from decrepit. The selectmen still came for the most part from among the most wealthy quarter of the townsmen. As in the past, long service in lesser positions brought them to office wise in the ways of the town and mature in years. For the burdens of the office were still great enough to require that a selectman be wealthy enough to have time free, and have age and experience enough to command obedience. Membership on the board carried a justified aura of dignity, and it was not good form to subject either the institution or its members to abuse. In their remaining discretionary powers as in their right to make up the initial agenda for each town meeting, the selectmen still possessed ways of exercising a discreet leadership over the actions of the town. At most, the final effect of all the changes was a redressing of a balance of power which had originally been tipped in favor of the selectmen. The town had moved from a pattern of politics which emphasized strong leadership toward a pattern characterized by a balance between executive efficiency and firm popular control. This was no more than what had been latent from the beginning in the theoretical powers of the meeting, though it had taken almost a century to bring theory into effective practice.

* * *

Perhaps what had happened in Dedham was no more than a random swing of the pendulum of local power toward the town

10. *Records,* IV, 214. See also Mann, *Annals of Dedham,* 80.

meeting. In the English parishes upon which the New England Town was modeled, the locus of power tended to migrate back and forth between the board of vestrymen and the parish meeting, depending largely on the local circumstances within each parish.[11] Perhaps Dedham had just experienced the first of what were to be many such casual alternations within its similarly bifurcated power structure. Yet the circumstances of Dedham's transition indicate that what was taking place here was something more fundamental and more general. The causes of the shift toward wider popular power in Dedham were similar to, and in some respects identical with, the causes of change which were simultaneously fragmenting the community. They were general causes stemming from the historical evolution of New England. If such causes were bringing greater popular power to Dedham, they may have been doing so in other New England towns. And, tied as it was to massive historical changes, the shift toward popular power may have been in some sense irreversible.

This is not to say that every potential cause of political change arising from the historical evolution of New England necessarily played a major role in widening the base of politics in Dedham. Some broad trends which may elsewhere have increased the power and activity of town meetings—statutory changes in the legal framework of the township, for example, or a widening of the local suffrage and increasing economic differentiation and conflict—had little effect here. Beneath them lay other trends which did the most to bring the new politics to Dedham and which were still more central to the evolution of New England.

Thus it is true that the legal framework of the New England township was progressively altered by the Massachusetts General Court so as to place more power in the hands of the town

11. Sidney and Beatrice Webb, *English Local Government,* I, *The Parish and the County,* 39, 41n., 42–43, 173ff.

meetings. An act of 1692 affirmed that final authority on bylaws rested with the meeting; two years later the Court transferred the privilege of electing assessors from the selectmen of the various towns to the meetings; in 1715 town meetings were given the right to elect their own Moderators. But these acts covered only a few of the new powers assumed by the Dedham meeting, and several were passed after the townsmen had already begun to exercise the powers in question. They had begun to elect a Moderator several years before the act of 1715 was even proposed. As far as Dedham was concerned, the legislature helped bring the meeting to power more through confirmation than through leadership.[12]

One other legal step taken by the General Court could possibly have sparked a trend to town meeting power. Scores of newly enfranchised men swelled the ranks of Massachusetts' town meeting voters when, in 1691, in response to mounting pressure, the Court lowered the local suffrage qualification from eighty to twenty pounds of taxable estate. In Dedham the law dramatically raised the proportion of men eligible to participate in the decisions of the meeting from forty to over seventy percent, and thereafter the percentage remained between sixty and ninety, always much higher than in the last years of the Puritan period.[13] Since this legal revolution put the town meeting firmly

12. *Acts and Resolves . . . of the Province of Massachusetts Bay* . . . , I, 65–66, 166; II, 30. See also *Records,* V, 87 (1712). Actually, the General Court's changes in the township law probably reflected an earlier change in grass-roots sentiment and in local practice, so little weight should be given to the trend of the law as a primary cause.

13. The suffrage analysis is based on tax lists in *Records,* IV, V, VI. Cook, "Transformation," 30–32, confirms this analysis and discusses fluctuations in the level of suffrage. For the laws, see *Acts and Resolves . . . of the Province of Massachusetts Bay* . . . , I, 2–20; and B. Katherine Brown, "Freemanship in Puritan Massachusetts." A better source for interpretations of the laws, and for information on the pressure for a wider suffrage in the 1680's, is Richard C. Simmons, "Studies in the Massachusetts Franchise," Ph.D. dissertation, University of California, Berkeley, 1965.

in the hands of the mass of men, it would seem plausible that it was they who awoke the meeting from its slumbers and made it the instrument of the popular will. However the mere expansion of the voting membership is not enough to explain the new assertiveness of the town meeting in Dedham. For twenty years in the heart of the seventeenth century (1648–1670) sixty to ninety percent of adult men had been eligible to vote, yet the meeting had remained dormant. Broad popular participation alone had not been enough then to give it life, and what broad participation alone could not accomplish then it could not be expected to accomplish later. Besides, the town meeting reached the peak of its power several decades after the reopening of the suffrage. Why should it have taken so long for the meeting's added voters to make their influence felt? The only conclusion is that the causes of the shift in the balance of power must lie else-where than in this expansion of the meeting's base. A substantial popular majority was probably a necessary condition of the shift, but that was a condition which could be taken for granted throughout much of Dedham's history.

It could be that the meeting's new members did more than restore the usual popular majority. It could be that the particular group of small farmers admitted in 1691 formed the core of a special interest group with grievances which led it to want to seize the meeting and through the meeting to dominate the town. No ordinary voters, they could slowly have assembled a majority and could have consolidated their control during the decades following the expansion of the suffrage. Here again the possi-blity must be discounted, at least as far as Dedham is concerned. As of 1691 there existed neither the sectional nor the economic divisions that give rise to such interest groups. The sudden influx of voters merely returned the meeting to the undiffer-entiated mass of farmers whose participation was an almost con-stant feature of town politics. Even at the end of the hundred years, economic changes had barely begun to fragment the society into interests whose antagonisms might one day generate political conflicts.[14]

Nonetheless, the proper sphere of causation does lie beneath the fluctuations of the law and in the evolution of the society. Gradually through the years immediately following 1691 the Dedham community, like most other New England towns, was aging, growing, and dispersing across the land. In their cumulative effects these changes hold the key to the refocusing of power in the town meeting.

The first of these events is already familiar. The circumstances peculiar to founding a town in New England early in the seventeenth century had combined to create an artificial aristocracy in Dedham. Before, during, and shortly after the settling of the town, a small number of men had emerged from the mass. Often they or their fathers had been among those who had come to America possessed of a little more wealth than the average immigrant, which gave them a temporary distinction that caused them to be called upon to take the lead in the difficult early days. Several were distinguished by their roles in obtaining recognition of the prospective township and in writing its Covenant. Others, serving among the first selectmen, had helped put that Covenant into practice. All were the beneficiaries of the ideology of the day, an ideology which encouraged continuing voluntary submission to the able and experienced few. As a result, these men and four or five of their immediate protégés were elected repeatedly to the board of selectmen, which they made the focus of power within the town. They were an "artificial" aristocracy because their dominance rested chiefly on their prestige as founders of this utopian venture and on continuing popular recognition of that prestige. Certainly none came of aristocratic

14. See also the next chapter. Again, as is the case in most particulars of the transition, the same is true of Watertown. See Lockridge and Kreider, "The Evolution of Massachusetts Town Government."

family, and none acquired the superlative wealth of the aristocrat while in America.

By 1690 hardly one of these men was still politically active, and by the turn of the century virtually all were dead. Their passing meant the end of the enforcement of the policies of the Covenant, but it meant more than this. Because no younger men could match their unique distinctions, and because no equally small and well-defined aristocracy of wealth had yet arisen to assert a comparable influence over the townsmen, the dying out of the founders' aristocracy had opened the board of selectmen to a wider range of men and removed much of its prestige. The way was open for the meeting to assume the leadership once held by the board.

There may have been more positive forces behind the disappearance of the old guard. The townsmen had done much to create the aristocracy by repeatedly electing its members selectmen. Had they desired to continue that aristocracy, they might have given its sons or chosen successors the same support. They did not. Perhaps after two generations of intense belief the townsmen were losing their faith in the subordinating ideology of the past, and after two generations of New World security were losing the ancient fear of chaos. They were therefore content to let their artificial aristocracy lapse. As it disappeared, they began to nibble at its powers.

Simultaneously the growth of the population seems to have added to the fluidity of the political atmosphere in a number of ways. One obvious result of a larger population was a surplus of potential leaders. In a society with no established gentry, it was easy for any substantial farmer to hope to enlarge his standing by means of a political career. But the budding leader of men faced mounting obstacles in the persons of his cohorts. By 1736 a man who was a member of the most wealthy fifth of the taxpayers found himself one of fifty men of equal substance, as opposed to one of twenty-odd half a century before. Facing the doubling number of solid citizens were five selectmen's seats, instead of the seven of the past. Either some men would have to forego their claims to a political role or the distribution of power would somehow have to be widened.[15]

The increased turnover and recruitment on the board of selectmen were probably attributable in part to this increasing supply of qualified men. The town could reject an incumbent, fully confident that it would be able to find a suitable and indeed eager replacement. The ready availability of men of substance actually led to a few contests, as several candidates challenged an incumbent for the town's approval. For those men who were not elected selectman as often as they desired, or who were never elected, the town meeting became an alternative route to prestige. There a man with a ready wit could stand out from the group with a well-phrased query. As the town learned to respect his views, he might be appointed to an *ad hoc* committee and find himself in a position to influence town policy. By making the meeting their means of political expression, these men were helping to make it the center of local politics.[16]

It is even possible that many of the ordinary townsmen may have become increasingly alienated from the board of selectmen as its members dwindled to an ever smaller minority of each

15. Tax lists in *Records,* V, VI. Since the standard of living was at least constant, the level of wealth implied by status in the top fifth of taxpayers was constant. The level was around 300 pounds in the currency of 1700, and is the level at which donations to needs outside the needs of the family increase sharply in men's wills, implying that this is the level at which comfortable support is reached. For a similar hypothesis concerning the effects of a surplus of leadership, see Clarence L. Ver Steeg, *The Formative Years 1607–1763* (New York, 1964), 129ff.; and Bernard Bailyn, "Politics and Social Structure in Virginia," in James M. Smith, ed., *Seventeenth-Century America: Essays in Colonial History* (Chapel Hill, N.C., 1959), 90–115.

16. This is based on a survey of the men who served on *ad hoc* committees, on the audit committee, and as Moderator. The electoral contests spoken of took place, of course, within the context of the sectional tensions discussed in the following pages.

generation. In the early days of the village one man in three would be a selectman at least once in his life; now not one man in six would ever occupy the office. Once virtually every man had a relative or neighbor or friend currently in the office; now it was possible to know a selectman as a reputation instead of as a person. For all the town's recruitment of new men, the far larger growth of the population was pushing the selectmen toward abstraction. Townsmen who had no wish to put their trust in impersonal authority could have made the town meeting the vehicle of their suspicion.

One last development channeled the effects of an expanding population into events which brought the town meeting to the fullness of power. It was not enough that the maturing society had shed its founding aristocracy; not enough that the old village had become a provincial town of a thousand souls.; it was also required that the population should disperse and then coalesce into conscious subcommunities. In a backhanded way the emergence of sectional tensions put the seal on the new initiative of the town meeting. Many would-be leaders and alienated townsmen finally rebelled, not just against the board of selectmen, but against a board and indeed against an entire town government controlled by the old village. They did not necessarily care whether that government was run by the selectmen or by the meeting. Ultimately they sought only the right to have their own towns, smaller units in which the old political harmonies could be restored. But in seeking to win that right they had to gain or force the approval of the Dedham government. In the process they brought before the town a flood of issues far too important to be left to the selectmen. Who would be the new minister? Where would the meeting house be located? What about the schoolhouse? Should Walpole be allowed its independence? Should Springfield? Should Clapboard Trees? Ordinary inhabitants with deep interests at stake insisted that the issues be debated in public. The resulting migration of power to the town meeting was confirmed in 1727, when the rebels captured the board of selectmen without gaining lasting control of the meeting, only to discover that they had won nothing. The town meeting which they had stirred into life with their contentions was no longer the creature of the selectmen. It had a mind of its own.[17]

The exact influence of each of these causes can never be known. The changing popular attitudes that may have encouraged and were definitely encouraged by the disappearance of the artificial aristocracy, the political dynamics of a growing population, the debates set off by sectional tensions—it is only certain that, combined, these did a great deal to bring about the ascendance of the Dedham town meeting. And this is enough, for what is of importance is that these were all causes which in essence transcended the accidents of local politics. These causes arose from New England's growth out of a collection of tiny Puritan communes to a provincial society of thriving, multiplying country towns. It can even be granted that the General Court's alterations in the statutes on local government, the widening of the suffrage, and tensions arising from a maturing economy might in spite of all the evidence have played an essential role in increasing popular power in Dedham. These causes, too, were tied not to the peculiarities of any one town but to the historical evolution of New England. Here as nowhere else in the Western world of the time, scores of towns were emerging from an artificial social and economic infancy and facing the consequences of an exploding and dispersing population, all under a government that placed considerable potential power in the hands of a majority of the townsmen. These were the historical winds of

17. And in the process the rebels also accounted for much of the increased turnover and recruitment on the board of selectmen. In both effects (strengthening the meeting, weakening the board), the sectional battle is inextricably mixed with the surplus of leadership and popular alienation ascribable to simple population growth. The latter causes could have, and for a time probably did, operate alone, but the former lent them direction (if oblique) and energy.

the time and place; what they did in Dedham, they could easily have done in many other New England towns.

* * *

Of course, on looking not just at the emergence of the town meeting but at the whole series of changes which struck Dedham in the early eighteenth century, one of these general causes stands out as the one that did the most to shape the history of Dedham and may therefore have had the greatest influence in other towns. Time and again the story of change returns to the sectional crisis created by the growth and dispersal of the population. As has been seen, the crisis first shattered the unitary community and then froze its fragments into a new kind of community. In the process it freed the townsmen to enjoy, or forced them to accept social and religious diversity. Simultaneously in the intertwined realm of politics the crisis was instrumental in widening the popular role in politics and in leading men to a new mode of political behavior.

This last point, by the way, cannot be too strongly emphasized. Dedham's new political style really had two elements, of which the shift in the institutional balance of power may have been the less significant. In the long run what mattered most was that men had changed their political behavior. The ambitious leaders of the sections had contended for popular support. Alliances were formed, broken, and formed again. Behind the alliances must have lain any number of caucuses in dark if not in smoke-filled rooms. Proposals were prepared, as were slates of candidates and petitions to higher authorities in case the candidates should fail or the proposals be rejected. The right to vote became important, so important that one faction was willing to break the law in order to extend that right. After some thirty years of such tactics the episode ended in a political horse-trade that gave each faction something and no faction everything of what it had sought. Men then settled down to the subtler politics

of power within a fragmented system. An entire generation had
left behind the experience of their progenitors and passed into an
age in which the majority, not the concensus, ruled. Essentially
without the economic differences which some social theorists
later claimed were necessary, a generation of men had nonetheless fought the classic campaigns of the democracy of diversity.
Among their leaders were men whose political skills compared
well with those of politicians of the Jacksonian era.

For the time being the larger significance of the new experiences generated by the sectional crisis remained as obscure
in the political realm as in the communal. No theorizer had
stepped forward to argue that society should be directed by the
will of a majority of adult males, each of whom would vote as
his interests directed, just as no one had come forth to define
the ideal society as one in which diverse communal and religious
groups would live side by side and in which every man could
choose among these groups according to his preferences. Nor
for that matter had the effects of the sectional crisis been enough
to turn the town *de facto* into a highly fluid or radically democratic society. But the town had come a long way since the days
of monolithic corporate quietism. In leading the men of the town
to alter both their communal traditions and their political behavior, the sectional crisis had done much to supply the experiential foundations of a new ideology.

* * *

Though profound, the effects of the sectional crisis were not
without their contradictions. Even before the crisis erupted
there had been signs that power was gravitating from the town
toward higher authorities. After 1675 local taxpayers began
paying more money to the county and colony than to Dedham,
as the former called for ever larger revenues to finance their
expanding activities. Following 1691 the town became notably
more careful in observing the procedural niceties demanded by

the law, knowing that the newly watchful county court would fine it for any error. Also, it seems that the decline of the tradition of local arbitration led increasing numbers of men to go to the county court to settle their everyday differences.[18] Augmenting these trends came a thickening snowfall of petitions precipitated by the sectional battles. The petitions did not result in a direct surrender of local power, but they did testify to the incompetence of the town in the face of the new problems and to the townsmen's growing willingness to beg higher authorities to solve those problems. Such evidences of failure could only have encouraged the authorities to continue their glacial encroachment on the power of the towns. And the precinct system imposed by the General Court certainly eroded the local authority from below by removing from the town much of its power over education, religion, and taxation, as well as much of the loyalty that had made the town strong.

The end result was a system of authority which spread the powers of the old corporation over a whole hierarchy ranging from the precinct to the town to the county court up to the General Court—and in theory all the way to the King of England. It was a system in which the townsmen customarily removed their disputes from the exclusive control of the corporation and sought solutions by appealing those disputes up through the hierarchy. For the town meeting the paradoxical consequence was that it had gained control of the town just as that institution lost its near-monopoly in the governance of the man on the land. What the crisis had given on the one hand, it had helped take away on the other.

There is a higher contradiction revealed by the town's passage through the sectional crisis. The myth of the New England Town is really a blend of two images. One is the peaceful, loving, and comfortable village in which men share an unspoken con-

18. Tax lists in *Records,* III–VI; manuscript court records in the care of the Clerk of the Suffolk County Clerk and in the office of the Clerk of the Superior Court, Boston.

sensus. The other is the town of the vigorous public meeting, where any farmer can get up, speak his piece, and stamp out in anger if he is not heeded—perhaps to get his musket. The lesson of Dedham's history is that the two components of the myth are incompatible. The events which brought an active democratic behavior to Dedham were the very events which destroyed the consensual community. Men who have the democracy of diversity must also accept the vocal and sometimes violent conflicts that give rise to that kind of democracy. It is pointless for them to wish for the ease of perpetual consensus, unless they envision withdrawing from the whole in a doomed effort to restore the homogeneity of the past. Whether they liked it or not, that is the lesson the Dedham townsmen had to learn.

8

Toward a New Society?

IN THE INTRICACIES of its evolution the history of Dedham most resembles a piece of music—and the themes of change were coming to dominate that history. But beneath change in inevitable counterpoint ran the theme of inertia, ever strong in any rural society.

Looking back over the century ending in 1736, there could be no doubt that inertia had prevailed, at least on that level of life on which men were born, fed themselves, and died. To the graybearded townsman of that year the clangor of the sectional crisis would have seemed mere noise heard over the processional of daily existence, a processional which, to judge from the past, would sustain itself endlessly and unaltered on into the future. Gradually it would become evident that amidst all the noise the old sense of community had disintegrated, opening to men new modes of communal and political behavior. Still later other and more fundamental changes would overwhelm the even pace of the old material existence. Meantime, at least the economic and social life of the town seemed to move on largely according to the measures set down in the days when the founders had cultivated their gardens under the rule of peace.

The weight of the past could prevail largely because the town remained so isolated. As the town's first hundred years drew to a close, emigration and immigration were almost as limited as they had been a generation or more before. Held by the web of affection, or by the expectation of a landed inheritance, or by sheer inertia, eight of every ten men born in Dedham would live out their lives and die there, still oblivious to the continent that waited to the westward.[1] Multiplying their collateral branches, almost never emigrating *en masse,* seldom dying out entirely, the families to which these men belonged epitomized the continuity of the society. As of 1728, thirty families dating to 1648 or earlier still included a majority of the town's population. To be sure, there was some slight erosion of the established stock—thirteen of the fifty-seven family names present in 1688 had disappeared by 1728; and there was an increasing dilution of that stock, as witness the thirty-one new names which appeared in the same period. But only very gradually was the grip of the many-branched elder clans being loosened by such infrequent disappearances from the ranks and such occasional arrivals of isolated newcomers.[2] For some time the clans would provide a stable social universe into which both new faces and new ideas could be absorbed.

1. See Lockridge, "The Population of Dedham" for estimates of gross decennial population mobility between 1680 and 1733. The figure of eighty percent is a minimum, and is based on a narrower study of men born in Dedham circa 1680–1700, carried forward to include emigrations up to 1760. In this case, emigrants not born in Dedham and emigrants "moved" merely by the secession of their part of the township have been deducted from the gross emigration estimates; otherwise, the techniques and sources are basically those used in Lockridge, "The Population of Dedham." The absence of large-scale emigration is confirmed by developments discussed in the latter half of this chapter.

But, while the improving quality of the sources for this later period does permit such relatively detailed inquiries into the movements of the population, it should be strongly emphasized that, before 1691 at the earliest and perhaps before circa 1730, the sources are still too weak to permit more than highly educated estimates. The situation becomes even more difficult when these estimates are compared with the still more unreliable and imprecise estimates for the earlier period. All that can be said for this, as for similar studies cited below, is that the available information indicates few significant breaches in the rules of continuity and isolation. (Such significant indications of change as do emerge will be considered in a later portion of this chapter.)

2. The thirty oldest families still accounted for a majority of the population because they, like all the indigenous population, had repro-

The town's enduring isolation was economic as well as demographic. As had their fathers and grandfathers before, the men of the early eighteenth century drew their substance from the surrounding lands. And a simple substance it was. The typical townsman was still an independent farmer who grew enough for subsistence plus a little for trade. He did not speculate in lands beyond the town borders nor did he contract with Boston merchants for large deliveries of foodstuffs. Though Boston's appetite was growing as its size increased and its trade in New England provisions spread throughout the Atlantic, the hunger of the city and of the larger world of international commerce had not yet altered the little cosmos in Dedham, only ten miles away.[3]

At least at the top of the spectrum, the simplicity of the economy was still mirrored in the distribution of the town's taxable wealth. The richest five percent of the townsmen were still no more than well-off farmers with a few attendant millers or innkeepers, and they owned only about fifteen percent of the property; the richest ten percent of the townsmen owned but twenty-five percent. This was exactly as it had been in the lifetimes of the founders when the emigrants had come from England with a vision of social perfection. Through the intervening years several of the cities and towns nearby had moved toward a more inequitable concentration of wealth in which a mere five percent of the men controlled nearly a third of society's assets and a mere ten percent controlled a majority of those assets, but

---

duced rapidly, and because the thirty-one newest "families" included a number of single men and newcomers who were the sole representatives of their names. It was for these reasons, too, that the new immigrants, though greater in absolute numbers than immigrants before 1688, caused only a small increase in the level of immigration relative to the whole indigenous population (from about .7 percent a year 1648–1688 to about 1.5 percent 1688–1728).

3. Again, the inventories in the Suffolk County Courthouse list names and quantities of crops, area and locations of landholdings, and most outstanding debts and credits.

in this respect Dedham's relative equality had been preserved in the amber of isolation.[4]

Indeed, as of the first outbreak of the sectional crisis back in 1704, the basis for a conflict of economic interest or class had hardly yet existed either at the top or at the bottom of the economic spectrum precisely because of this isolation. At the very beginning of the eighteenth century Dedham had been far from idyllic, and the townsmen had begun to find ample reasons for contention—conflicts of communal identity, even of communal property, of religion to a degree, of personal ambition certainly —but so far they had been spared the warfare of interest against interest and class against class.

Contained within the town, all the old rhythms of life recurred by day, season, year, and generation. Born into a family with four or five children, the mythical "average" man would marry in his middle twenties and die in his fifties. He would know little of plague and less of famine. He might live in a house with one room more than his father's house, might own an ox or loom or piece of pewter more than had his father, but the odds were heavy that he would succeed to his father's lot in life. Often literally, if he were an eldest son, for he stood to inherit the familiar homestead and to take up his father's time-worn plow upon the fields round about.[5]

For all that it may have been boring, the old way of life was still not bad. Few young men fled the will of the patriarch

4. For Dedham, the sources are inventories, and tax lists (*Records,* IV, 2–4, 19–23, 94–96, 292–97, 360–65). For other towns, see J. T. Main, *The Social Structure of Revolutionary America,* chapter 1; and James A. Henretta, "Economic Development and Social Structure in Colonial Boston." In terms of the wealth of the top ten percent of men, the figures would be twenty-five percent for Dedham as against fifty percent in some other cities and towns.

5. Lockridge, "The Population of Dedham," discusses the continuity of vital demographic characteristics; inventories reveal the standard of living; wills and inventories of succeeding generations establish dependence on inheritance and reveal patterns of inheritance. The spatial, occupational, economic, and social mobility of the young men of this generation (born 1680–1700, died 1700–1770) will be discussed in the text and footnotes that follow.

and the ways of the past.[6] The man who stayed had the comfort of the familiar. He and his compatriots would probably enjoy a standard of living approximating that of their fathers, their town's total wealth having grown tremendously as the tracts of virgin land kept their promise through three ever larger generations. If, when the time came to choose an occupation, a local boy still followed in his father's footsteps, usually becoming a farmer and thereafter achieving modest wealth very slowly, the cause must not be misunderstood. It was not because men of entrenched wealth or privilege had shut out other avenues, but because of the continuing simplicity of the economy. Within its narrow limits a youth was nearly as free as ever to move from job to job and upward to wealth as fast as energy and diligence would take him. When and if he attained the pinnacle of local wealth, he would not find it a disgrace to be known as "farmer" or "smith" or "miller." [7] Or so it seemed.

* * *

Yet time would not leave the town forever turned in upon itself, moving to these measures of the past. Looking *ahead*

6. As noted above probably no more than two of every ten men born in Dedham 1680–1700 would emigrate (before 1760). Many of these left after appearing on the tax lists as adult males (24 or over), only the remainder leaving as boys or young men. Some of these latter no doubt left involuntarily when their families emigrated. All in all, it would be safe to say that no more than ten percent of native youths living in early eighteenth century Dedham *decided* to seek their luck elsewhere. (The percentage was always higher in wealthy, better-connected families.)

This narrative has little to say about family structure because the nuclearized semi-extended families which Philip Greven found in seventeenth-century Andover ("Family structure . . . in Andover") were characteristic of Dedham through the early eighteenth century. Since there was no change, and since the social implications of this sort of family structure have not been worked out (and it is a very ambiguous structure), nothing has been said about it.

7. Exact occupational mobility is hard to obtain, since it is exaggerated by a superficial increase in the specificity of occupational self-labeling in the years 1680–1740. A check based on the tools and debts listed in the inventories of succeeding generations (as well as on

from the perspective of 1736 it was possible to predict another wave of change, this one extending far into the settled patterns of the economy and of the society. Despite the many evidences of continuing isolation, simplicity, and homogeneity, certain small alterations in the conditions of life were already apparent by this date. Extrapolated through the next fifty years these promised to take Dedham into a world of ever more complex social harmonies and, perhaps, dissonances.[8]

Many of the signs pointed to the further opening of the society to the possibilities introduced by the sectional crisis: to action, diversity, and choice. There was even a suggestion of equalitarianism in the air. As late as December of 1728, the tax lists had still begun with names of several distinguished citizens —Captain Samuel Guild, Mr. Seth Dwight, Widow Judith Richards—in accordance with a custom begun by the rank-conscious Englishmen who had founded the town. Then in August of 1729, the next list began, "A: Captain William Avery, Widow Sarah Aldis, John Aldis, Nathan Aldis. C: Benjamin Colburn, Nathaniel Colburn Senior . . . ."[9] All at once the tax lists no

---

self-applied occupational labels) indicates that *at least* seventy-five percent of sons continued in their fathers' occupations, a percentage slightly but not greatly lower than in previous generations.

The absence of evidence to the contrary, together with recurrent cases of rags-to-riches and riches-to-rags found by tracing men through a sequence of tax lists, and a study of self-labeling by the very richest men, establishes the absence of artificial limits to social mobility. Defined purely as the opportunity to acquire wealth, the social mobility of "third generation" young men (born circa 1680–1700) did not differ greatly from that of their fathers. In the aggregate, the two groups took roughly the same number of years to reach the same standard of living. The percentage of sons who became indisputably more wealthy than their fathers was virtually the same in both groups. But the size of the available sample is small and the ambiguities of defining relative wealth are great in this case, so any conclusions are inevitably weak.

8. For the evidence which justifies the extrapolation of these trends (in Dedham and in other towns), see K. Lockridge, "Land, Population, and the Evolution of New England Society, 1630–1790," *Past and Present*, no. 39 (1968), 62–80.

9. *Records*, VI, 292, 302.

longer reminded men of their obligation to defer to age, service, and wealth. Was it just for the sake of administrative convenience that henceforth every man's position on the list would depend solely on his rank within the alphabet? Possibly, but the fact that in this case convenience had prevailed argues that the already bedraggled custom of social precedence was giving way to a *de facto* assumption of equality, at least when equality had convenience on its side.

Judging from the numbers of townsmen now engaging in lawsuits, any new sense of individual equality must have been a vigorous one. The old tradition of local mediation had been based on a passive notion of equality in which men were equally bound to keep the peace of the collectivity. The jousting in the public courts which had replaced that tradition demonstrated an every-man-for-himself equalitarianism that was nothing if not aggressive.[10]

In the years preceding and above all in the years immediately following 1736, new economic opportunities were arising from the steady growth of the population in and around Dedham. A farmer with a knack for leather-work set aside his plow to help his neighbors with harness or boots, until finally so many came for help that he stored the plow and became a tanner. A man with a capacious wagon took orders for merchandise whenever he left on a trip to Boston, until at last the orders came so thick and fast that he filled his front room with the usual goods of the storekeeper. A landholder began to see that the increase in the population would one day create a demand for his surplus land, so he quietly purchased more land in the towns of the area. The traffic on the road from Boston to New York encouraged a

10. The beginnings of the custom of public litigation can be traced in the Suffolk County Court records mentioned in chapter 4 (footnote 13). Edward M. Cook, Jr., "Social Behavior and Changing Values in Dedham, Mass., 1700–1775," unpublished manuscript, 1968, 31–32, confirms the continuation and increase of the practice into the 1770's.

widow to make of her house the town's second inn. After three
generations of improving business, the local millowner and his
relatives were acquiring shares of grist mills throughout the
region, amassing the capital that would build a textile empire
in the early days of the machine age.

Thus the ways to wealth were sure to multiply, and some
of these ways promised to lead to considerable wealth. All the
more reason for a clever young man not to leave town. Even
if he had no capital, the opportunity need not go begging, for
soon a few men with more funds than their occupations could
absorb would make a new business of judicious small loans.[11]

Profit was no respecter of boundaries. As with the shop-
keeper, the speculator, and the millowner, the enterprising
townsman would find that the demands of trade forced him into
ever more contacts with the world outside. What a passion for
profit was doing for some men, the lure of love or of education
was doing for others: an ever larger proportion of local eligibles
found brides and grooms in other towns; and, while before 1705
only three sons of Dedham had graduated from Harvard, by
1737 eleven more had taken degrees and passed into the ranks
of the provincial intelligentsia.[12]

The slow rise in immigration brought in more bits and pieces
of the outside world even while more townsmen were reaching
out into that world. The tax lists caught a growing number of
transients and single newcomers, strange names from God knew

11. The wills, inventories, and deeds in the Suffolk County Courthouse permit the reconstruction of individual and family economic
histories. Some of the transitions described, and the practice of
specializing in small loans, date from the years immediately after
1736. See also Lockridge, "Land, Population, and the Evolution of
New England Society."

12. Mann, *Annals of Dedham;* marriage records for Dedham in
Records, I, and for neighboring towns in the *Vital Records* series of
the New England Historic-Genealogical Society; and Cook, "Social
Behavior and Changing Values in Dedham, 1700–1775," 30.

where with God knew what hidden in their pasts.[13] No doubt the selectmen kept a close eye on this miscellany, but not close enough to keep many a Dedham boy from learning far too much about the fascinations of the wilderness, the city, or the seas beyond the town line.

If these signs had any meaning, the trend of the future seemed to lead to a society in which the individual took advantage of an increasing range of choices while facing a decreasing range of restrictions. Yet the signs were deeply ambiguous. It appeared that the future would bring restrictions of its own and that the new age would not be altogether golden. This is not merely to say that the cosmopolitanism and individualism of the ultimate future would fill men with longing for the isolation and simplicity of the past. Well they might, but the way to the future promised more material disadvantages more immediately.[14]

Once again the source of the trouble lay in the relentless logic of growth. Because the diversification of the economy was slow and because for some time there would be no revolution in the means by which goods were produced and transported, the fortunes of most of the next three or four generations of townsmen would rest with the land. And it was the A-B-C of Dedham's future that the supply of land was limited while the size of the population was not. By 1736 the falling away of Medfield, Wrentham, Needham, Bellingham, and Walpole had reduced the township to a quarter of its original area. Within the contracting boundaries the population had risen to about 1200

13. Lockridge, "The Population of Dedham," and tax lists in *Records,* VI. See also Footnote 2.

14. Again, the signs of change discussed here and the picture of the future derived from them are confirmed, and are extended to other towns in the area, in Lockridge, "Land, Population, and the Evolution of New England Society." Cook, "Social Behavior and Changing Values in Dedham" confirms many of the particulars and the general trend of the evidence.

souls by 1736. At that rate the shrunken town would contain 1600 souls by 1750 and over 2000 by 1775.[15] Since Dedham could expect no compensating grants of land from the neighboring towns, all of which had to provide for swelling populations of their own, only large-scale emigration could ease the mounting pressure. For various reasons this would not come about, and the population would go on rising. At some point there were going to be too many people for the land to support. Whatever effects of the collision were not already visible could have been anticipated by a man with no special gift for prophecy.

The milestone at which an abundance of land became an impending scarcity had already been reached. For seventy-five years the proprietors of the town lands had accommodated their proliferating posterity by reaching into their reserves for "dividends" of five, twenty, or seventy acres. With the dividend of 1713, those reserves ran out.[16] From this point on the families of Dedham could no longer multiply confidently on into a future blessed with gifts of free land; they would have to provide for coming generations out of their existing holdings.[17]

These holdings were not as extensive as might be supposed. The estate of the typical first-generation farmer had included nearly 150 acres, more than he could use. Out of this patrimony and continuing dividends of public land, his sons had made estates as large or larger. Now, early in the eighteenth century, his grandsons were down to around 100 acres apiece, for the skein of dividends was ending and they had drawn most of their substance from their fathers' estates. Although plenty for their needs, in the absence of further dividends this number of acres

15. And it did reach these levels. See Lockridge, "The Population of Dedham."

16. *Records,* VI, 126.

17. Of course, the problem this posed varied with the original proprietary share of each family, and with its abilities to add to its holdings through purchase. But, since very few families made extensive purchases outside of town, the local land-pool was fairly self-contained, and all families faced the problem of scarcity to one degree or another.

would not be enough to take care of those who would follow. By the end of the eighteenth century the grandsons of these grandsons could expect to inherit no more than fifty acres, not enough to support a family.[18]

The prospect was darkened by the fact that the few acres inherited by a man of the fifth generation might not have much life left in them. The rich river-bottom lands of the earliest divisions would be worn out after a century and a half of primitive farming. Some were already "worn" in 1736. Most of the lands parceled out in the later divisions never had much life in the first place. They had been divided only under the pressure of the growing population and, when put to the plow, they quickly gave up their rocky best.[19]

18. The 150-acre figure is based on public land divisions, 1636–1660 (*Records,* III–V); the under-100-acre figure is from Suffolk inventories; the under-50-acre figure is from tax lists in volume CLXIII of the state Archives (1786).

The only available studies indicate that, in rural areas of colonial America with soils as good as or better than those of Dedham, a minimum of sixty to ninety acres was required for a farm which would sustain five or six persons and provide a small surplus (though the area of a viable farm was no doubt lower in areas deeply involved in the market-cash-crop economy, which Dedham was not). The total is so high because of the need to leave some land "resting" fallow every year, and because extensive pasture area and woodlots were required; only five to thirty acres would actually be under cultivation in a given year. See Charles S. Grant, *Democracy in the Connecticut Frontier Town of Kent* (New York, 1961), 36–38; and James Lemon, "Household Consumption in Eighteenth-Century America," *Agricultural History,* XLI (1967), 59–70.

19. The text, above and below, discusses the lack of change in Dedham's agricultural practices, which, as the inventories show, were essentially exploitative, involving little use of fertilizers or legumes. This was typical of New England; see Percy Wells Bidwell and John I. Falconer, *A History of Agriculture in the Northern United States, 1620–1860* (Washington, D.C., 1925). The increasing appearance of "worn" land in the inventories confirms this analysis. As for the more recently divided lands, the fact that these were reserved until the last speaks for their quality. One dividend in 1690 was canceled because the land was not worth the price of surveying (manuscript land records, Town Hall).

Moreover, the rising demand which had brought on the cultivation of these marginal lands had also begun to force up the prices of the better arable land faster than the general price level.[20] Eventually the land-hungry horde which was stripping the worst lands would bid the best out of the market, forcing most men back upon their meager inheritances.

So, paradoxically, almost impossibly, by 1736 Dedham faced the prospect of scarcity in the midst of the potentials of the New World. Apparently the long-ago emigration of their great-great grandfathers was not going to leave the members of the fifth generation materially better off than their counterparts in England.[21] Instead they were destined to encounter the age-old worry of men living in villages where there was not enough to go around: "What will become of us, of our children?" And they were fated to live in a society not unlike the structured societies of land-hungry Europe.

While the lives of most townsmen had not yet been touched, already by 1736 enough men had been affected by the mechanism of scarcity to produce measurable changes in the local society. Because some families felt the pinch before others, there were already men with small landed inheritances who struggled to save money with which to buy the additional land that would enable them to marry, to support their families in decency, and to bequeathe independence to their sons. Despite their best efforts, they were being left behind as the value of their labor and even of their crops was outdistanced by the rising price of land.[22] What could a man do? Caught on the horns of this

20. This is an extrapolation from price data in inventories, cited in Lockridge, "Land, Population, and the Evolution of New England Society." See Footnote 22.

21. An English yeoman (of the previous century) had farmed lands ranging in area from 25 to 200 acres; Mildred Campbell, *English Yeoman*, 74–100.

22. Until a systematic study of differential (land vs. crops vs. other goods) price rises in colonial New England is available, the mechanism suggested here must remain somewhat hypothetical.

dilemma, he might have no choice but to sell his few acres and try something else, or go somewhere else. Thus it was that, though for some time emigration was to remain too low to relieve the economic pressure significantly, the number of men leaving town had begun to increase. While at first glance these few emigrants might seem to signify a more mobile society in which men chose among new alternatives, from a more realistic perspective such mobility and choice were the products of conditions that were beginning to force men everywhere to uproot themselves and wander in search of the opportunities they could no longer find at home. Evidently the emigrants did not find easy solutions elsewhere. If they had, news might have gotten back and set off a greater exodus, which did not happen.

Most victims of scarcity chose not to venture on the unknown. They stayed on, and began slowly to accumulate as a sort of lower class. The share of the town's wealth owned by the poorest twenty percent of taxpayers had already fallen from almost ten percent circa 1690 to five percent circa 1730. In practical terms this meant that the collective standard of living of the lowest fifth of the society had descended from one of near-independence to one of scrabbling inadequacy. The hard core of this group were the landless, who in the same years had increased from five to over ten percent of all taxpayers, and were still increasing. One man in ten had as assets little more than his strong back; how long before it would be one in five? Simultaneously the numbers of abject poor thrown on the mercy of the town rose faster than the rising population, and there began to appear among the usual widows, orphans, idiots, and cripples men whose strong backs had availed them nothing. So many names were added to the relief rolls that for the first time the townsmen began using the collective term "the poor," signifying their awareness that the shadowy subclass found throughout Europe since written memory had now sprung up in Dedham. In the future this class would wax considerably (the town had to build a poorhouse in 1771), much later it would wane, but it would not go away. It was the societal version of original sin.[23]

Even a decade after the end of the hundred years the tax lists still gave no hint that an equivalent upper class was arising. The share of the town's wealth being lost by the poorer sort was meaningful only to them; it was as yet too small to raise significantly the twenty-five percent of wealth owned by the ten percent of men at the top. In any event it was taken up evenly through the rest of the spectrum.[24] Still, the mechanism which was pushing down a class of "have nots" was reciprocal; someday the demand for land would vastly enrich those who still had plenty.

Meantime, entirely without engrossing a larger share of the wealth, a kind of upper class was just beginning to emerge. The more prosperous local farmers were finally beginning to drop the traditional "yeoman" in favor of "gentleman." [25] Though their relative wealth had not increased (and though numbers of them had not seen nearly enough public service to merit the distinction on that basis), they obviously felt justified in assuming this title and their neighbors and the officers of the state accepted their claim. Why? The hypothetical example of one such man, Daniel Fisher III, shows why. Not wealthier or more respected than his father, Daniel Fisher could become a "gentleman" to his father's "yeoman" because time was on his side. Time brought

23. This is *taxable* wealth and land, which included nearly all of each; tax lists in *Records,* V, VI. (A few of the landless taxpayers who had extensive personal property have been excluded from the ranks of the landless-as-poor). The standard of living is from inventories. References to individual cases of relief and to "the poor" are found in *Records,* V, VI. Mann, *Annals of Dedham,* cites the Town Hall manuscripts concerning the poorhouse.

24. It is possible that the emergence of a wealth-monopolizing (to state the extreme case) class was hidden by the initiation of the practice of under-assessing the property of the rich, a practice not unknown today.

25. Deeds, wills, and inventories reveal the change in nomenclature. By 1775 it had embraced nearly ten percent of the society.

him into a world more impressed with England and with men's social differences than with Puritanism and the community of the saints. Time placed him in the third instead of the second generation of his prominent family, giving him that much more of the first prerequisite of a gentleman, a distinguished family history. Time brought him to maturity at a moment when a small but increasing number of men were unable to guarantee the welfare of their descendants, giving the old wealth passed on to Daniel a new meaning. He could still take care of his own, possibly more than that if he used his cash legacy to speculate on the rising price of land. The distresses of that moment also freed him from working with his hands by offering a growing pool of poor laborers. He would have more leisure for his affairs or for a little genteel politicking in the village. Thanks to the times, then, Daniel Fisher and others like him could make good their claim to be an American equivalent of the Old World gentry. And it is indisputable that a group which identifies itself and is identified as a superior class, is.

Before long, accelerating geographical segregation would make the differences between these developing classes all the more apparent. As the junior branches of old families were forced out onto marginal lands, and especially as poor newcomers were shunted out onto the same lands, the population of the outlying precincts would become biased toward poverty. By 1750 these areas contained seventy-five percent of the poorest fifth of taxpayers, but only sixty percent of the total population. Men from senior lines of old families tended to stay in the village, where their inheritances of the best land and local businesses were located, so its forty percent of the population was weighted with sixty percent of the wealthiest tenth of taxpayers.[26] Two distinct social environments were emerging, one characterized by scattered dirt farmers struggling to stay off the poor list, and the other dominated by gentlemen long accus-

26. This is from tax lists in *Records,* VI, and in the Town Hall manuscripts.

tomed to the best of everything available and to the ebb and
flow of the tiny metropolis. What had been at best a faint under-
current at the beginning of the sectional crisis would become
a measurable reality by the middle of the eighteenth century.

By the time this happened the rich could be further distinguished from the poor by their political rights. As their fortunes waned, poorer men slipped below the level of property
required of voters. Between 1720 and 1750 rampant inflation
raised the paper value of virtually all estates above the required
level, heading off the spread of disenfranchisement. But when
a recoinage in the latter year restored the old values, it turned
out that a quarter of the adult taxpayers did not hold the property necessary for a vote in provincial elections.[27] From all indications this quarter would expand toward a third and on toward half as the population and the land continued to collide.
(The proportion of men qualified to vote for local officers also
fell, though it remained at a slightly higher level because the
property qualification was a little lower.)

As the eighteenth century moved on toward its end, as the
generations increased and remained within the town and their
legacies shrank apace, the polarization of the society would
intensify. The social legacy of scarcity would be widespread
poverty, a distinct class consciousness, and substantial disenfranchisement. Though it would never take the town into conditions as extreme as the worst in Europe, the process of overcrowding would push conditions a significant distance in that
direction. Thus the society of the town in the years around 1736
was deceptive in its apparent continuity and tranquility. It had
already started down the road toward a series of potentially
devastating changes.

*   *   *

27. See note 26, above, and chapter 7, for the relevant sources
and laws. The figure of twenty-five percent allows a seven percent
margin of error. See also Lockridge and Kreider, "The Evolution of
Massachusetts Town Government."

There was a disturbing air of fatalism in the way the townsmen were submitting and would continue to submit to crowding and to its consequences. Neither was entirely inevitable; in theory many things could have been done to avoid both. Why were these things left undone, as by and large they were? In understanding why, one comes to see how the townsmen could be so imprisoned by the forces of historical inertia that they were unable to reverse the process which was eroding their opportunities and polarizing their society.

As long as men insisted on staying within the town, their shrinking holdings could have been made to support a family by the adoption of new agricultural techniques such as mixed fertilizers or crop rotations focused on legumes. These would have restored the land, increased yields, and could eventually have made some farms smaller than fifty acres viable. But these techniques were not introduced until very late in the eighteenth century, if at all. In the first place, if all the efforts of gentleman experimenters and pamphleteers could not revolutionize the agriculture of England until the later eighteenth century, how could more be expected of these remote New Englanders? Besides, three generations of "dividends" had allowed careless habits to come to the fore to a degree rare in England; when there was always more land, there was no need to lavish care on existing holdings. By the time that scarcity demanded better husbandry, this carelessness had hardened into tradition. It would have been no simple matter to convert men to new techniques, even had the preacher been available. Finally, there was reason to doubt that some of the town's farmlands could have responded sufficiently even under the best of husbandmen to make fifty acres yield more than the narrowest margin of subsistence.[28]

Small landholders could also have raised their incomes by specializing in the crops which brought premium prices in Bos-

28. See Footnote 19.

ton. The wheat from a fifty-acre farm, taken to the booming
capitol, might have earned the farmer and his family a year's
subsistence. This expedient, too, was not adopted, probably
because it, too, was not a real possibility.[29] Dedham was only
ten miles from Boston, but within an arc of ten miles around that
city were half a dozen closer towns, all doubtless eager to supply
its demands. Along the Atlantic shore to the north and south
were another dozen towns more accessible by water than was
Dedham by the rutted roads of the day. Anyway, from the evidence of the crops stored in Dedham barns at harvest-time, the
soil was better suited to rye and Indian corn than to wheat.

If the land would not support them, men might become
artisans, and make rope, shoes, tools, beer, and cloth for their
neighbors. Some did, more as the century wore on.[30] But someone had to buy their goods if they were to live. A town in which
the standard of living was if anything falling could not be
expected to support many artisans. More extremely wealthy
men would one day emerge to employ more artisans and also
more agricultural laborers, somewhat widening these alternatives,
but never by enough margin to solve the town's problems. And
in any event, these were undesirable alternatives for formerly
independent yeomen to face. They would be converted to occupations in which they depended upon other men for their existence. They, and any farmers who were able to specialize in
crops for the urban market, would enter a commercialized world
in which men's relationships were at once enhanced and polluted
by ties of economic dependence and in which all men became
prey to ruin by speculative collapses.

But the one question which recurs throughout the town's
tale of mounting woe is: Why *did* they stay? If the scarcity was

29. Again, crop and trade data are from inventories.
30. Occupational surveys based on inventories, wills, and deeds
show an increasing proportion of artisans, though this may be deceptive,
for reasons given in Footnote 7, above.

becoming so acute and the local alternatives were so few, what kept them there? Some did leave, of course, but never enough to do more than slow a little the process of crowding. That so many should stay under such conditions seems incredible to our impatient age. Yet as has been seen, circumstances made emigration neither an easy nor an effective alternative for the individual townsman. Again, for every lure that urged a man to leave town there was a force which held him there. In the days before the telephone and the airplane, anyone who left his home and family was likely to lose all contact with them for long stretches of time. To emigrate might mean abandoning the old climbing oak, the hearth, relatives and childhood friends—all the small-town familiarities. It also meant leaving the only sure sources of care in time of need, one's family and one's native town.

The custom of partible inheritance was one of the strongest of the forces holding young men within Dedham, and the weight of inertia is nowhere more clearly seen than in the failure to discard partible inheritance despite its inappropriateness under the new conditions. In the old days the certainty of a fair share of the family lands, which had held sons within the town, had also been a promise of more-than-sufficiency. The generations were thereby united within a stable social order in which all had a likelihood of comfort. But as the numbers of each succeeding generation increased and the landed legacies began to shrink, the continuing assurance of a share in an estate helped hold men within the society only at the price of overcrowding that society. It might have been better to have replaced partibility with primogeniture, to have given all the family land to the eldest sons so that they could have had prosperous farms and to have left their brothers small cash and walking shoes. By sacrificing some of its posterity, the town could have preserved a healthy level of opportunity for those who remained. Unable to be this ruthless, attached to tradition, fathers (and in cases of intestacy, the law) went on offering the emptying promise of partible inheritance to each larger generation.[31] Preferring a small certainty at home to a large possibility elsewhere, each grasped at that certainty, stayed, and the town moved on toward economic crisis. In the end the continance of the old custom could not even salvage social unity by sacrificing economic opportunity, for sooner or later hopelessly small legacies of land must hound many sons into flight. Appropriate to the spacious past, partible inheritance lived on after it had outlived its usefulness and become pernicious.

Of course, what made the familial warmth and small legacies of Dedham most attractive was the dismal prospect facing the would-be emigrant. He must go out to live among strange people, and in towns which had no legal obligation to aid him in moments of distress. To the east, all around, were towns with population problems of their own. Westward new towns were starting, but instead of giving land away their proprietors were selling it, so a prospective townsman had to arrive with cash in hand.[32] In many of these townships the soil was better left to lichen than turned to crops. In some a scalping, burning war party could be expected whenever the Indians decided to try to rearrange the frontier. It is no wonder that no émigré found a promised land and sent back word for his fellow townsmen to join him.

31. Partible inheritance (see chapter 4) was still the custom in most wills and the law in cases of intestacy. Only toward the end of the eighteenth century was there a trend toward primogeniture in wills and a tendency on the part of the courts, in the case of small intestate estates, to give all land to the eldest son and have him pay off his brothers in cash from the profits of the farm, which had thereby been kept intact and viable; Suffolk Probate and Court Records, as cited previously.

32. See E. V. Greene and V. Harrington, *American Population before the Federal Census of 1790* (New York, 1932); and Bidwell and Falconer, *A History of Agriculture in the Northern United States;* again, Lockridge, "Land, Population, and the Evolution of New England Society;" and Roy Akagi, *The Town Proprietors of the New England Colonies* (Philadelphia, Pa., 1924).

Where else could a man turn? To war, to the oldest device of all for draining surplus young men. The Imperial wars of the eighteenth century would come at an opportune moment. Enticed by this deadly adventure more than by the scanty opportunities elsewhere, some impoverished young townsmen would march off to battle. Here in Dedham, in the land of opportunity, the cannon fodder was ready.[33]

*   *   *

The ironies of the town's evolution had now become inescapable. From the day the policies of perfection had fallen into disuse, the townsmen had begun to cast off the old collective passivity. They went freely into court to assert their individual claims against their neighbors. Each showed up at the town meeting to defend the concept of community which he thought ought to prevail, and so together they remade the meeting into the arena of a new politics based on their contending interests. They came to expect the right to attend or even to form a church whose minister voiced their particular convictions. They were gradually turning Dedham into an open society where diversity prevailed and the majority truly ruled. More, they were moving toward an age in which the free individual would move among a vast array of choices—legal, political, religious, occupational, geographic—and would be enshrined as a new kind of god. The logical next step in this process was for men to begin breaking free of the last ties of the old community, ties that bound them to their fathers' occupations and held them within the environs of the town. This would require the emergence of varied economic

33. The Suffolk wills and inventories reveal that, with each war, scores of not very well off young men from the old county towns made their wills and went off to war, many not to return. Indeed, if one assumes that for every man who died in the war (i.e. left a will which was soon after probated and which states his intention to join the fray) nine more returned safely, the numbers involved must have been quite large.

opportunities both within and outside the town, of substantial social and geographic mobility which would let the local society open up to the fullest, leaving the individual maximum leeway to shape his destiny within the town or to leave it and seek his fulfillment elsewhere. Yet this next step was blocked.

And there was the irony: Prepared by events for a continued opening of the society and for wider choices for the individual, the townsmen were destined to encounter instead the continuation of the old immobility and the actual deterioration of economic opportunity. And, in a particularly cruel irony, the vigorous popular politics born in the sectional crisis were soon to be eroded by the decline in eligibility for political participation imposed by the economic crisis. History seemed to be contradicting itself.

The tension created by this contradiction of trends was to have its historical function, however. Politically, at least some men would be able to see a clear need for an ideology which would guarantee every individual the right of participation. The radical ideologues of the American Revolution would supply that need and some men in Dedham would respond. Socially, many men would be ready to acclaim a government which would open new economic opportunities to the individual. The new Federal government would do that, especially under the direction of Thomas Jefferson and his Republican party, and again some men in Dedham would respond.[34]

In this way eighteenth-century Dedham was to enter the main stream of subsequent American history. If a mere list of specific features were to be made, it would be hard to say that the town of 1736 was more "American" than the village of 1636. For a European social ideology the town had exchanged the beginnings of an opportunistic individualism that might possibly be called American, but for its early and very American

---

34. For events in Dedham in this later period, see Frank Smith, *History of Dedham,* and James M. Smith, *Freedom's Fetters: The Alien and Sedition Laws and American Civil Liberties* (Ithaca, N. Y., 1956).

abundance and economic equality it had exchanged a most European trend toward scarcity and stratification. It is the *dynamics* of its features that made the provincial town more typical of the main currents of American history than the old village. In the village, utopianism and abundance had combined harmoniously, for a time. But there could be no harmony between the rapidly developing individualism and the social Europeanization of the eighteenth-century town. Only dissonance, only tension, out of which would come men clustering about a liberty pole and, later, migrating west under the aegis of a republican government.[35]

As with the sectional crisis, the crisis of overcrowding depended on circumstances which could have shaped the history of other New England towns. In the latter case these included the reluctance to emigrate, the prevalence of the custom of partible inheritance, and the adherence to a relatively primitive agriculture, which could hardly have been features found only in Dedham. And though their effects on men were essentially at odds, both the sectional crisis and the crisis of overcrowding arose above all from the steady growth of the population which was most definitely typical of New England at large. So the way the lives of the Dedham townsmen were affected by the succession and interplay of these crises could have been echoed in scores of other towns, and the irony of Dedham's history thereby enlarged.

* * *

The story has gotten ahead of itself in following the trend toward overcrowding so far into the eighteenth century. As of 1736 the town was hesitating on the brink of this development

35. In a broader perspective, of course, what happened in Dedham was the further disintegration of a closed corporate peasant community more or less as predicted by Eric Wolf in "Closed Corporate Peasant Communities in Mesoamerica and Central Java." But this disintegration came with unusual intensity in Dedham because of the very fervor of the town's original utopianism. And the blend of social "opening" and individualization with overcrowding that occurred here was peculiar (i.e., not a necessary part of Wolf's theory) and did create unusual tensions.

and on the brink of the contradictions and tensions which it would bring. Again, the essential feature of Dedham's first century was the weight of a past whose roots reached back into the history of medieval Europe. Only subtly, only slowly, only inadvertently were changes in the various spheres of life coming together to lay the foundations of a new mode of existence. Yet as long as the momentum of the story of change has carried the narrative well past 1736, it would be well to mention that other crises in other spheres or life, crises unquestionably common to many New England towns, brought further changes to Dedham even as the crowding was intensifying. The effect of these crises was to heighten the tension between individualism and the growing lack of economic, social, and political opportunity.

In the 1740's the preaching of Jonathan Edwards and the arrival of George Whitefield electrified the colonies into a revived awareness of the awesome God of Calvinism. In Dedham this Great Awakening (as it was generally known) helped rekindle the intense pieties of the old congregations. Yet as elsewhere, the religious disagreements engendered by the revival pushed the town a little farther along the road to multiple denominations. By inviting the townsmen to debate the meaning of God's Word and to choose among churches and sometimes even among politicians representing various interpretations, the Great Awakening took them another step toward the age of individualism.[36]

For a time the dissolution of higher authority in the early stages of the American Revolution would invite the towns once again to see themselves as autonomous bodies within which men would make utopias sufficient unto themselves. In some towns the effects of the Revolution went little further, but in most the Revolution went on to stretch men's political consciousness from

36. See Alan Heimert, *Religion and the American Mind from the Great Awakening to the Revolution* (Cambridge, Mass., 1966); Alan Heimert and Perry Miller, eds., *The Great Awakening: Documents Illustrating the Crisis and Its Consequences* (Indianapolis, Ind., 1967); and Cook, "The Transformation of Dedham, Massachusetts."

the town to the state, and beyond, to the nation. From this point one could foresee the day when the once all-embracing town would subside as political existence in America came to be polarized between the individual and the nation. Revolution also brought at last an ideology that would justify, nay glorify, individual rights. Armed with this ideology, any man could demand the right to vote.[37] But the fulfillment of the demand would take decades. For the moment, in Dedham, the American Revolution could only heighten the tension between individual expectations and the real lack of opportunity by raising the former to a new high without substantially increasing the latter.

It was not until the early nineteenth century that the opening of the society and the liberation of the individual would reach a culmination in Dedham. Just as the crowding became acute, the weakening impulse to stay would be overwhelmed by the attraction of cheap, rich soil in the Ohio Country. Many of the "new men" shaped by the events of the eighteenth century would stream out of Dedham to join their compatriots from other towns on the way West. At the same time the town would thrive in its new roles of county seat and summer home of Boston aristocrats, and suffrage reforms would bring nearly universal manhood suffrage, keeping the promises of the Revolution. Then, with the Industrial Revolution of the 1830's and 1840's, the economies of Dedham and of New England at large would undergo another upheaval and men would move in and out under the imperatives of a national economy. It only remained for the forces of the later nineteenth century to bring the tides of immigrant laborers who would revivify the society and open it still further to diversity, and to convert the old farmlands into businesses and homes for commuters to Boston.

All the same, the hard rock of the past would never be

37. See Robert Taylor, *Massachusetts, Colony to Commonwealth: Documents on the Formation of Its Constitution, 1775–1780* (Chapel Hill, N. C., 1961), for examples of all these effects.

eroded entirely by these forces. Something of the village of 1636 would remain to the present day. The town meeting is still running local affairs, though the selectmen have regained the initiative. There is still among many inhabitants a strong sense of belonging, of "us" in the town as against "them" out there. This has happened because, for all the opening of the society and the eagerness of some individuals to embrace the opportunities offered by change, there were always men who would stay on and keep alive the desire for unity and order.

III

Dedham and the American Experience

Insofar as the history of one New England town cannot be repeated in the history of any other, the story of Dedham must stand alone as one atom of our national experience. But clearly Dedham was not entirely unique. The forces which most shaped the history of this town—the residual peasant outlook and Puritan social ideal of the founders, for example, or the later growth and dispersal of the population—were general forces which must have affected other towns. Hence, in its main features the story of Dedham could well have been the story of many New England towns and so of much of early America. In this sense the history of one town can and should be used to illuminate the larger history of its times and nation.

To what extent was the history of Dedham actually duplicated in other towns? To a great extent. And what does the illumination which Dedham's history, thus enlarged, provides, reveal about the American experience? It reveals that this part of colonial America was moving away from a powerful corporate impulse deeply indebted to the European past, toward an age of pluralism, individualism, and liberty. Yet in the end the history of this and of its companion towns also suggests that the evolution of a libertarian society in America was neither as rapid nor as direct as might be thought.

9
Dedham and
the American Experience

〰〰〰〰〰〰〰〰〰〰〰〰〰〰〰〰〰〰〰〰〰〰〰〰〰〰〰〰〰

IN ITS CONSCIOUS corporate utopianism Dedham was in the mainstream of a wide and enduring New England tradition. The impulses which led its founders to create that social synthesis were in fact common to the founders of nearly all the towns in the first waves of New England settlement. In many towns overt corporate utopianism did prevail, at least for a time. Covenants were written and signed. Policies of social planning and exclusiveness were undertaken to implement those covenants. In practice as in theory local politics tended to fall into the mode of voluntary conservative corporatism that was necessary to the success of the utopian synthesis. Local society evinced a simplicity, stability, and patriarchalism that further guaranteed its preservation.[1] While in some towns the synthesis was weak and

1. For the typicality of various general aspects of earliest Dedham, see Page Smith, *As a City upon a Hill: The Town in American History* (New York, 1966); Michael Zuckerman, "The New England Town in the Eighteenth Century" (Ph.D. dissertation, Harvard University, 1966); John Coolidge, "Hingham Builds a Meetinghouse," *New England Quarterly,* XXXIX (1961) 435–61; William Haller, Jr., *The Puritan Frontier: Town-Planting in New England Colonial Development, 1630–1660* (New York, 1951); Richard L. Simmons, "Studies in the Massachusetts Franchise"; Kenneth Lockridge and Alan Kreider, "The Evolution of Massachusetts Town Government"; and Philip Greven, Jr., "Family Structure in Seventeenth-Century Andover, Massachusetts," *William and Mary Quarterly,* XXIII (1966), 234–56. See also John J. Waters' recent "Hingham, Massachusetts, 1631–1661: An East Anglian Oligarchy in the New World," *Journal of Social History,* I (1967–1968), 352–70.

Admittedly, these few works cannot constitute final proof of Ded-

quickly disintegrated, and in others it was unable to resist powerful divisive forces,[2] the extraordinary tranquility of New England's rural society throughout much of the seventeenth century
testifies to the fact that in most towns the elaborate system
designed to produce peace, unity, and order remained intact for
at least a generation. Even later, after time had hopelessly
eroded the overt synthesis in most towns, the old ideals of peace
and unity were invoked in town after town. Beyond the eighteenth century well into the nineteenth, townships splitting off
from older towns or newly founded in the wilderness would
sometimes write covenants, echoing that desire for communal
perfection which had been the guiding spirit of earliest New
England.[3]

In this light it would seem that the power of the American
environment to transform human society has been exaggerated.
Thousands upon thousands of the earliest Americans turned
their backs on the wilderness. Aided by the fact that the material
and social opportunities of the New World were not so great as
to overpower all social coherence, they refused to let its un-
deniable abundance spin them outward into the incoherence of

---

ham's typicality on this point. But there are as yet few integral
studies of the early New England town, and virtually none of the
scholars involved has cared to think in terms of systematic utopianism
or in terms of the peasant outlook that is an element in any rural
utopianism. [Since even Arthur Bestor, *Backwoods Utopias, The Sectarian and Owenite Phases of Communitarian Socialism in America,
1663–1829* (Philadelphia, Pa., 1950) gives short shrift to the utopianism
of the first New England towns, other scholars can hardly be blamed
for following suit, or indeed for stressing the weakness of the utopian
impulse, as does Sumner Powell, and as does Daniel Boorstin in the
The Americans: The Colonial Experience (New York, 1958).] So,
until scholars with receptive minds study a number of early towns,
the works by Smith, Zuckerman, Coolidge, Haller, Simmons, Kreider,
and Greven, will have to suffice to raise even if sometimes indirectly
the possibility that Dedham's utopian experience was typical.

2. See Sumner Chilton Powell, *Puritan Village;* and Darrett B.
Rutman, *Winthrop's Boston* (Chapel Hill, N. C., 1965).

3. Again, see Page Smith, *As a City Upon a Hill: The Town in
American History.*

individual opportunism. In searching for a social ideal with which to shape the first layer of a new history, they looked back to the ideals of the past. These ideals encouraged men to strive for perfection, but defined perfection as peace, unity, and order. Because they were successfully implemented, for decades life in this part of America was intimately linked in all its phases to the intellectual and social traditions of medieval Europe and to a worldwide peasant tradition dating from the origin of recorded history. So persistent was the desire to define social perfection in terms of stability, so satisfying was the achievement of that desire, that elements of the communal ideal derived from the past remained alive in the towns of New England and of the northwestern territories of the United States even after the passing of Jefferson and the coming of Andrew Jackson.

This deepest layer of the American experience was in every way conservative. It was conservative in that it looked to the past for wisdom. It was conservative in that the substance of the wisdom it found in the past was skepticism: that in a world inclined to chaos the most men could hope for was a stable life within a small community. It was conservative in that the outlook it created resisted change long after it had become obvious that the skeptical lessons of the past did not entirely apply to America, after it was clear that opportunity and individual freedom within a fluid national society could be achieved without fatal disorder. On this conservative foundation a large part of the history of our nation has been constructed. In the depths of the American experience lies a craving for peace, unity, and order within the confines of a simple society. Though it is not à la mode to say so, next to it lies a willingness to exclude whatever men and to ignore whatever events threaten the fulfillment of that hunger.

But there were in this earliest age the seeds of a more optimistic America, which after the further evolution of the national experience would burst into flower. At first the re- markably pervasive utopian impulse, an impulse that on one occasion could weld a hundred strangers from diverse parts of England into the social organism known as Dedham, was inseparable from the conservatism of the age. But time would leach away some of the conservatism, leaving a widespread desire for perfection and the belief that it was to be found in America. Then it would matter that at least some part of America had possessed from the beginning an ingrained utopianism, a utopianism not just of leaders or visionaries but of the common man. The optimistic visionary Thomas Jefferson would find awaiting him a number of believers in an American utopia, whose confidence would help make of him the leader of a national political machine dedicated to the realization of a utopia of opportunity and freedom. Similarly the initial abundance of land and the economic equality which it fostered, together with the relatively wide base of political participation characteristic of this part of early America, would take on new significance after the time of Jefferson; they would cease to be the accidental or subordinate parts of a synthesis which looked to the past, and would become instead the dominant elements of a new synthesis which welcomed the future.

*   *   *

This is skipping too far ahead, however. Between the seventeenth century and the nineteenth America went through an intricate process of change which paved the way for the new values of the Jeffersonian and Jacksonian eras. Insofar as it is typical, the history of Dedham can help to explain how the Americans of New England moved away from a uniquely intense conservative corporatism toward an acceptance of a uniquely optimistic vision of individual freedom.

By and large Dedham was an accurate mirror of a process which began with the beginning of settlement and which by the middle of the eighteenth century had brought New England out of the Puritan matrix and prepared it for the libertarian ideology of the American Revolution.[4] Throughout New England "the close-knit, tightly controlled community of the earlier period became steadily more open and heterogeneous; [New England] was moving toward a new social order, toward the republican pluralism of the nineteenth century . . . [experiencing] the growth of liberty."[5] A multitude of historical forces affecting every sphere of life were combining to work this transformation. Once the Puritans were in New England, safe from the persecutions that in England had united them, their religious differences grew into open disagreements. These festered for generations, until the Great Awakening brought them to fever pitch while adding new causes of religious conflict. The existence of open disagreements within the ranks of the ministry weakened popular

4. The major proof of Dedham's typicality in this respect comes from an excellent book by Richard L. Bushman, *From Puritan to Yankee: Character and the Social Order in Connecticut, 1690–1765* (Cambridge, Mass., 1967). The manuscript of *A New England Town* was nearly complete when this work became available, hence the two books are entirely independent, yet their views of the process of change are largely similar. (The extent to which the author disagrees with Mr. Bushman or refines his conclusions will be made evident in the final section of this conclusion.)

Other works indicating to one degree or another Dedham's typicality in this respect are: Michael Zuckerman, "The New England Town in the Eighteenth Century" (though he would disagree with many of the immediately following conclusions, his study provides much evidence that can be used to support them); William Haller, Jr., *The Puritan Frontier;* Richard L. Simmons, "Studies in the Massachusetts Franchise"; Kenneth Lockridge and Alan Kreider, "The Evolution of Massachusetts Town Government"; Philip Greven, Jr., "Four Generations: a Study of Family Structure, Inheritance, and Mobility in Andover, Massachusetts, 1630–1750" (Ph.D. dissertation, Harvard University, 1965); Charles S. Grant, *Democracy in the Connecticut Frontier Town of Kent* (New York, 1961); John M. Bumsted, "Religion, Finance, and Democracy in Massachusetts; the Town of Norton as a Case Study" (paper delivered at the Iowa University Conference on Early American History, March, 1967); Kenneth A. Lockridge, "Land, Population, and the Evolution of New England Society, 1630–1790"; and Jackson Turner Main, *The Social Structure of Revolutionary America* (Princeton, N. J., 1965).

5. Richard L. Bushman, *Puritan to Yankee,* ix.

respect for the established Puritan church and for the political
leaders who supported that church. The growing spectrum
of religious opinions invited every man to free himself of the
dictates of the establishment and invited him to select his own
form of Christian belief, or to eschew belief altogether. At the
same time the economic opportunities of the New World tugged
at ever more members of the Puritan communities, inviting them
to flock into the cities to seek worldly success, and tempting
those who achieved it to imitate the manners of the English
merchants who were their models. Opportunity pulled others
away from established society, tempting them out into the
wilderness to seek furs or new land, urging them to give free
rein to the speculative impulse that must sooner or later dominate a rapidly growing society placed on the edge of an un-
tapped continent. All the groups thus emerging—the varied
religious groups as well as the merchants and land speculators—
naturally sought political influence in order to buttress their
opinions or enterprises. Some failed, some succeeded. Together, by the middle of the eighteenth century, they had
shattered the old politics of Christian corporatism. In place of
obedience to a narrow clique of divinely ordained leaders they
had put a politics of diverse, frank, and contending interests.

The major arena of the transformation was the town. This
was the level of government which most affected and the level
of existence which most shaped the lives of nearly all men.
Entirely without leaving the borders of his community, a man
could participate in events which would bring to him and his
neighbors that experience of pluralism toward which the entire
society was moving. Even as the utopian concern initiated by the
first generation weakened, the growth of local populations led
to the division and assignment of town lands ever more distant
from the old village center. After a time, men heeded the voice
of mere convenience. They abandoned the web of relationships
created by residence in the villages in favor of farmsteads located
on their faraway holdings. Once there, a variety of motives

coalesced outliving farmers into groups dedicated to achieving a degree of legal independence. Some of these men only wished for the convenience of their own churches and schools, and perhaps for the increase in value which these might bring to their property. Others who were involved in the religious debates of the day hoped to place in their new church a minister who preached their own brand of divinity. Still others, the men who so often led their sections beyond a demand for parish or precinct status into a campaign for full independence as a new township, were moved by political ambition. Yet they were supported in turn by followers whose chief wish seems to have been to reconstruct in their locality a semblance of the original intimacy and order of the village from which they had emerged.

The divisive forces reached a peak in the years 1700–1750, when everywhere across the landscape of rural New England towns burst into heated political activity as outlying sections sought to separate and village centers resisted their demands. No matter what the resolution in each case, diversity had come to stay. In those towns which divided into parishes or precincts the diversity of religion and of political authority became permanent. And in nearly all towns affected, the sectional crisis created on the local level a politics of contending individual and group interests which replaced the old politics of silent consensus beneath an accepted leadership.[6]

Within the towns something of the ideology of the old communal order remained. Faced with an unprecedented crisis, all parties concerned repeatedly invoked the language of the Covenant.[7] They pleaded for peace, unity, and order with an almost

6. Richard L. Bushman, *Puritan to Yankee,* Appendix I; Michael Zuckerman, "The New England Town in the Eighteenth Century," which not only confirms the widespread existence of sectional crises in eighteenth-century Massachusetts, but establishes the typicality of Dedham's new style of politics (albeit inadvertently); and, again, Lockridge and Kreider, "The Evolution of Massachusetts Town Government."

7. Which fact is one basis of Zuckerman's contention that despite

desperate insistence. To no avail. Men were speaking and even
thinking in terms of an old ideology, but they were living a new
one. Whether they liked it or not pluralistic democracy was
replacing the democracy of homogeneity, freeing the individual
from the dictates of the social order, and laying the experiential
foundations of the ideology which was to become America's
pride.[8]

* * *

It would seem, then, that both without and within the towns
of New England the forces of historial change were altering the
influences of the past, rising in an irresistible flow toward freedom and democracy and creating the liberated American who
would elect first Jefferson then Jackson.

Yet, while there is a great deal of truth in such a view, taken
without qualification it is an historical fairy tale. The evolution
of Dedham and of the New England towns which it represents
can *also* be viewed from perspectives which indicate that the
process of historical change bringing America toward the present
was convoluted and ultimately cautious.

For one thing Dedham's history shows how the coming of
change within the towns depended to an extent on the very
persistence of a certain core of the old ideology. Again, one of
the motives leading groups of outlying farmers to seek independence was a desire to re-create their own corporate villages.

---

the stresses of the new age the former peace, unity, and order prevailed
in the towns of eighteenth-century Massachusetts. He cites also some
other evidence of considerable substance, and his contention has a certain validity, as will be seen from the final section of the conclusion
that follows.

8. This entire process, by the way, justifies a sort of neo-Turnerian
view of American history. If not the frontier as such, it was certainly
the rapid growth and consequent dispersal of much of the population
of New England which was *the* essential factor in bringing on the
democracy of pluralism within its towns (though not quite in the way
Turner envisioned).

But often the village center resisted their wishes in the name of the same corporate ideal.[9] Out of the disagreement between these two groups, each in some sense viewing itself as the defender of the old way and each desiring to perpetuate that way, came the battles which led all concerned into an experience of communal diversity and political activism that was entirely antithetical to the way of the past. Thus the future came to many towns, not because some men envisioned that future and set out to undermine the old order in the name of the new, but because changing conditions provoked contradictions in the old order which in turn tumbled men all inadvertently into new experiences.

It follows from this that the changes manifested in the towns of New England did not necessarily involve a conscious rebellion against authority. If in the end the authority of the social order as represented by the township was diminished, it was not because some townsmen had fought to reduce a degree of local authority they considered in principle excessive, but because their attempt to create new foci of that same authority in the form of new towns had led to disputes which unexpectedly paralyzed the local government. All inadvertently, without a man in town necessarily objecting to the tradition which vested in the townships great powers over the individual. If men obtained greater freedom, it was in some sense in spite of themselves.

It may not even be proper to speak of an actual diminution of authority. Authority over the individual was dispersed through a hierarchy of officials, from those of the Precinct to those of the town to the Justices of the Peace and of the County Courts up to the General Court itself, but the total amount of authority was probably no less than when the monolithic township had dominated the scene. While there can be no doubt that the new pattern of authority freed the individual by offering

9. Zuckerman, "The Massachusetts Town in the Eighteenth Century" provides much explicit evidence that Dedham was typical in this respect.

him more chances to appeal decisions and to play one locus of authority off against another, it would be premature to conclude that men had moved very far toward a future in which authority was minimal and was expected to keep its hands off the individual in all but the most necessary cases. A similar hierachicalization of the patterns of authority had taken place in seventeenth-century Europe, and Europe in the seventeenth century was far removed from the ideology of minimal government and individual liberty.[10]

For that matter, the entire process of change in New England looks considerably less radical when seen from a European perspective. Compared with the Europe of the seventeenth century, earliest New England began as a uniquely isolated, small, simple, devoted, united, corporative, orderly, and perhaps authoritarian society, a society characterized by an unusually intense utopian impulse which pervaded both the religious and civil establishments. Through the almost century and a half between its founding and the American Revolution that society matured. First the impossibly intense utopian impulse weakened of itself, and parts of the social synthesis arising from that impulse began to fall everywhere into disuse. Then religious differences and economic ambitions grew large enough to weaken the grasp of the already defensive leaders of the degenerating colonial establishments, while within the towns the forces of growth led to a politics of diverse interests paralleling that which was emerging on the colonial level. Finally, continued growth and the advent of land scarcity within many towns led to increasing social differentiation and to some extent to the acceler-

10. Sydney V. James, "Colonial Rhode Island and the Beginnings of the Liberal Rationalized State" (paper delivered at the Convention of the Organization of American Historians, Chicago, April, 1967), depicts in Rhode Island a similar passage from an "old régime" corporative system of authority to a "new régime" hierarchical system in the period 1680–1730. He derives his terms from the work of the European historian Emil Lousse, and he argues that the transition in Rhode Island parallels a similar transition which took place in Europe shortly before, a transition described by Lousse.

ated diffusion of the population through migrations. This was a process which, from a European perspective could be seen as no more than a return to normalcy.

For it could be said that *as of the middle of the eighteenth century* change had merely returned this part of America to much the same sort of economic, social, political, and religious pluralism that had been characteristic of England and to some degree of all western Europe since the end of the middle ages. After all, the events which had brought New England society from Puritan corporatism to the threshold of the Revolution had hardly turned it into a wild Jacksonian melee.[11] It did retain certain unique energies stemming from its utopian cast of mind, from its tradition of wide political participation, and from its relative social equality based on an abundance of land. But these qualities had sprung into being during the Puritan age, and though they were perpetuated during the subsequent process of pluralization, they were *not* essentially products of that process. Besides, by this time the utopianism was largely latent, the practice of wide participation lacked a vitalizing ideology and was threatened with erosion, and surprisingly few men of the time wanted to or were able to take full advantage of the abundance of land. In fact, the society had become in many respects comparable with the English society of its day. If the New England townsman now had a choice of religions, so did his English counterpart. If he now appealed his grievances up through a hierarchy of authorities, so did the troubled Englishman across the Atlantic. If he now saw politics as an arena in which he must prosecute his individual interests, so did his English brother, and had for some time. If now occasionally the heat of his concern led him to riot, riots were not unknown to his English equivalent. And around the American townsman were emerging the poor and landless just as in England, cared

11. And here is where Zuckerman's contention that the towns of eighteenth-century New England were still quite orderly becomes relevant; cf. "The New England Town in the Eighteenth Century."

for with laws duplicating the English poor laws. Emerging above
him were "gentlemen" who increasingly affected the superiorities
of the English gentry.[12]

So not only did the process of change as manifested in the
towns of colonial New England involve no deliberate rejection
of the past or rebellion against the idea of authority, but also
as it operated both within and without the towns it was not
fundamentally a process of Americanization. The uniquely
corporative America of the Puritans underwent what was in
effect an Anglicization before going on to the greater and
indisputably unique pluralism, democracy, and individualism
of Jeffersonian America. Only after being placed in the soil of
this resumed normalcy, then watered by the ideology of the
Revolution and given growing room by the exodus to the West,
would the seeds of a uniquely free America contained in New
England's history since the Puritan age rise to fruition.

With one exception. Because of the material with which it
started and because of its pace, the process did create a dissonance that went beyond mere Anglicization. No sooner had
change seized a closed Puritan society with submerged traditions
of social equality and wide political participation and re-enforced
those traditions with a growing pluralism that widened the range
of individual choices, than it faced that newly opening society
with an increasing scarcity of land, deepening class distinctions,
and a narrowing suffrage.[13] By the latter part of the eighteenth

12. The only work, American or English, which includes an
attempt at a detailed comparison between the American and English
rural societies of the mid-eighteenth century is Peter Laslett's *The
World We Have Lost,* and it does so only in passing. It is a pity
there are not more, especially in view of the tendency of historians of
colonial America to emphasize American uniqueness without any but
the most general (and often wrong) ideas about the nature of the
English society of the period.

13. Robert E. Brown, *Middle Class Democracy and the Revolution
in Massachusetts* (Ithaca, 1955), would disagree as violently with this
statement as the author disagrees with Mr. Brown's view that "middle
class democracy" characterized the towns of Massachusetts right up

century, the tension between these effects of the Anglicization of New England had given rise to a peculiarly intense consciousness of the fragility of equality and liberty. This consciousness would help lead some Americans to espouse a radical brand of revolutionary ideology that promised to guarantee both equality and liberty by reforming American society from within as well as by freeing it from the clutches of Great Britain.[14] But it was only in this backhanded way that the society of mid-eighteenth century New England was made distinctly more American by the events which were changing it.

It would be possible to go on in a spirit of caution and point out that even after the Revolution the emergence of the America of Jefferson, Jackson, and de Tocqueville was far from instantaneous. Nor was that developing America the unalloyed democracy of legend. Not simply surviving beside it, but mixed deeply into it was a large portion of the old conservative communal corporatism. The rabid localism of some Antifederalists, for example, partook as much of the utopian communalism of early New England as of the political radicalism of the Revolution.[15]

But the point should by now be clear. In American history as in the history of any nation the future came inadvertently, indirectly, and slowly. Layer was added to layer, they intermingled, and out of the mixture came the future, sometimes in the most unexpected ways. There has never existed the straightforward erosion of a pure past by a pure future. The philosophical point is important, and beneath it is a meaning for American

---

to the Revolution; see Kenneth Lockridge, "Land, Population, and the Evolution of New England Society."

14. Again, see Kenneth Lockridge, "Land, Population, and the Evolution of New England Society."

15. See Robert Taylor, *Massachusetts: Colony to Commonwealth,* for documents illustrating this kind of "revolutionary localism." This actual *alloy* of corporative, localistic past with mobile, individualistic future is treated to some extent in Page Smith's *As a City upon a Hill,* but is best perceived by T. Scott Miyakawa, *Protestants and Pioneers: Individualism and Conformity on the American Frontier.*

history: The American national character evolved indirectly, very slowly, and retained within itself much of its past. The embryonic Americans of mid-eighteenth century New England were Englishmen with a utopian hangover, some local traditions of equality and participation, a sense that these were being eroded, and a few resentments against clumsy Imperial officials. Enough to lead men into revolution, this was hardly enough to make of them the restless, seeking, insatiable "new men" later encountered by Alexis de Tocqueville. For all the preparation involved in the long years of colonial existence, Americans were finally revolutionized into the classic nationality of the nineteenth century by events which took place over a span of some seventy years following 1763. Even then they were never fully revolutionized, because at the base of their history, enduring through its transmutations and altering the character of each new synthesis, there remained a conservative impulse centered on the town and on the past.

Bibliographic Essay

~~~~~~

THIS IS A SELECT bibliography of the works which have contributed to the ideas evolved in this book, most of them evaluated within the framework of these ideas. Though not a comprehensive account of all works remotely pertaining to the New England Town, it is considerably more than a list of the items cited in the footnotes, and it includes all the most recent studies of New England towns.

SECONDARY WORKS: BACKGROUND:
MAIN FEATURES OF THE HISTORY OF NEW ENGLAND

A large number of books and articles have provided the general background on the history of colonial New England without which a study of the New England Town could neither begin nor, once completed, be used to illuminate the course of American history. The works of Perry Miller are indispensible starting points for every student of New England's Puritan origins: *The New England Mind: the Seventeenth Century* (New York, 1937) and *Orthodoxy in Massachusetts* (Cambridge, Mass., 1933) are particularly valuable in delineating the impulses toward perfection which motivated the founders of the several colonies; together with "The Half-Way Covenant," *New England Quarterly,* VI (1933), 676–715, they also reveal the stresses that soon developed within the resulting religious, political, and social syntheses. In *The New England Mind: From Colony to Province* (Cambridge, Mass., 1953), Miller takes up where *The Seventeenth Century* leaves off, suggesting the idea of spiritual decline as he reveals the intricacies of the evolving Puritan mentality.

An essential supplement to Miller's early works is Edmund S. Morgan's *Visible Saints: The History of a Puritan Idea* (New York,

1963), which is a fine account of the historical sources and practical details of the New England Puritans' attempt to create nearly perfect visible churches. Strangely, though, in his earlier *The Puritan Dilemma: The Story of John Winthrop* (Boston, 1958), Morgan focused more on Winthrop's pragmatism than on the utopian impulse which so clearly touched his spirit as he approached the American shore; but "The Puritan Social Ethic; Class and Calling in the First Hundred Years of Settlement in New England" (Ph.D. dissertation, Yale University, 1966), by Steven Foster, a student of Morgan, tips the scales by returning to and skillfully articulating the Puritan theory of social perfectionism that had so impressed Perry Miller.

Charles Lee Haskins' superb *Law and Authority in Early Massachusetts* (New York, 1962), and Richard L. Simmons' "Studies in the Massachusetts Franchise" (Ph.D. dissertation, University of California, Berkeley, 1966) discuss the execution in the areas of law and politics of the general perfectionist impulse perceived by Miller and further elucidated by Foster; these two books may be viewed as paralleling in the secular realm the job done by Morgan's *Visible Saints* in the religious.

To be sure, while they all at one time or another highlight the Puritans' utopian impulse, Morgan, Foster, Haskins, and particularly Simmons are as aware as Miller that the explicit social synthesis produced by that impulse was bound to disintegrate. Still, they do recognize the power of the initial drive for perfection, which is more than can be said for Arthur Eugene Bestor, whose otherwise interesting *Backwoods Utopias: The Sectarian and Owenite Phases of Communitarian Socialism in America, 1663–1829* (Philadelphia, Pa., 1950), virtually ignores the high Puritan age, or for Daniel Boorstin, whose brilliant and provocative *The Americans: The Colonial Experience* (New York, 1958) is stubbornly one-sided in its focus on Puritan pragmatism [1] and on the further pragmatism presumably imposed by the American environment.

Among the works which throw an oblique light upon this question of social utopianism are: Kai Erikson's *Wayward Puritans: A Study in the Sociology of Deviance* (New York, 1966), which suggests interesting methods of social analysis and reminds scholars of the sense in which the unique features of New England society can be isolated only when that society is viewed in the context of

---

1. The word is here used in the sense of a predisposition to practicality, not in the related philosophical sense of William James.

classic, universal patterns of human social behavior; Charles M. Andrews' *The Connecticut Intestacy Law* (Connecticut Tercentenary Pamphlet, New Haven, Conn., 1933); Edmund S. Morgan's *The Puritan Family* (Rev. ed., New York, 1966); and Emil Oberholzer, Jr., *Delinquent Saints: Disciplinary Action in the Early Congregational Churches of Massachusetts* (New York, 1956), which is a useful supplement to Erikson.

It was no easy task to pick up the multiplying strands of the declining Puritan synthesis, to follow them through to the eve of the American Revolution, and to show precisely how they and the new lines of development that entered with time merged into the beginnings of a new and more open social fabric; but Richard L. Bushman, *Puritan to Yankee: Character and the Social Order in Connecticut, 1690–1765* (Cambridge, Mass., 1967), succeeded to a surprising degree. In spite of certain shortcomings, his book is the model of the evolution of New England society in the late colonial age against which all others must be measured.

A host of studies served Bushman as a necessary foundation. Among these are Bernard Bailyn's "Politics and Social Structure in Virginia," in *Seventeenth-Century America: Essays in Colonial History* (Chapel Hill, N.C., 1959), 90–115, and Clarence L. Ver Steeg's *The Formative Years* (New York, 1964); Bailyn and Ver Steeg were among the first of modern scholars to take a broad, evolutionary view of colonial society, and though their shared interpretation of the nature and meaning of change does not necessarily harmonize with Bushman's, their view of the period 1670–1720 as a period of transition resembles his own. Roy Akagi, *The Town Proprietors of the New England Colonies* (Philadelphia, Pa., 1924), E. V. Greene and V. Harrington, *American Population Before the Federal Census of 1790* (New York, 1932), Edmund S. Morgan, *The Stamp Act Crisis: Prologue to Revolution* (Chapel Hill, N.C., 1953), Albert Laverne Olson, *Agricultural Economy and the Population in Eighteenth Century Connecticut* (Connecticut Tercentenary Commission Pamphlet, New Haven, Conn., 1935), John Miller, "Religion, Finance, and Democracy in Massachusetts," *New England Quarterly*, VI (1933), 29–58, and to a degree Alan Heimert, *Religion and the American Mind from the Great Awakening to the Revolution* (Cambridge, Mass., 1966), directly or by implication lend support to Bushman's portrait of an opening society.

But Sydney V. James' "Colonial Rhode Island and the Beginnings of the Liberal Rationalized State" (paper delivered at the meeting of the Organization of American Historians, April, 1967) implies that the eighteenth-century process of "opening" Bushman describes did not go so far as to constitute a real "Americanization" of the society. Taken together, James' approach and the evolutionary hypothesis contained in the works of Bailyn and Ver Steeg cited above could be said to describe a society which, in the years 1670–1720, was passing from a Puritan political order to a new political order. This transition arose in large part from the evolution of the artificially narrow Puritan society toward a certain degree of diversity, and from the attendant conflicts, which disrupted the old corporative politics. But James, Bailyn, and Ver Steeg make it appear that while the new legal-political framework that resulted was more flexible than the old, it was nonetheless stable, proto-aristocratic, essentially European in its characteristics, and in fact often oriented toward England. Could the newly opened New England society which that English-style, legal-political order was created to serve and so successfully contained have been much more open, diverse, perhaps anti-authoritarian, and in this sense more American, than the English society of the day? It seems doubtful, for if it had been, the new political order would have collapsed in turn, and one truly American would have taken its place—which did not happen until after the American Revolution.

Other works reveal that the steady growth of the population which was the major cause of the social "opening" Bushman describes may eventually have had opposite effects, leading to overcrowding and to social stratification. This fits nicely with the idea that what was really taking place was not yet a full Americanization but rather an interim Anglicization of New England society. Olson's *Agricultural Economy and the Population in Eighteenth-Century Connecticut* indicates that overcrowding did occur, as does Jackson T. Main, *The Social Structure of Revolutionary America* (Princeton, N.J., 1965), and as do several local studies cited in the appropriate section below. Perhaps Bushman made little use of this scattered evidence because he placed his reliance on the thoroughly researched but rather too broad thesis of Robert E. Brown, *Middle Class Democracy and the Revolution in Massachusetts* (Ithaca, N.Y., 1955) that eighteenth-century America was a "middle-class democracy" with plenty of opportunity for almost everyone. If he did, Bushman was not alone, for so, implicitly, did the more-experienced Bernard Bailyn, in "Political Experience and Enlightenment Ideas in Eighteenth-Century America," *American Historical Review,* LXVII (1962), 351. Their reliance on Brown can be explained by the fact that over the last half century virtually no one other than Lois

Kimball Matthews, *The Expansion of New England* (Boston, Mass., 1909) and Rowland Berthoff, "The American Social Order: A Conservative Hypothesis," *American Historical Review*, LXV (1960), 495–514, has been led to suggest quite explicitly that there was an increasing lack of elbow room in late eighteenth-century New England, to ponder the consequences of this development, and to wonder at its meaning for American history; no one has yet produced a comprehensive work on the subject. Gordon S. Wood, "Rhetoric and Reality in the American Revolution," *William and Mary Quarterly*, XXIII (1966), has recently if indirectly raised again the possibility that pre-Revolutionary society was not the opportunity-laden paradise of legend (and of Robert Brown), and has hinted that a growing lack of opportunity could explain why some Americans seem to have welcomed the Revolution against British authority as a fine chance to agitate for internal social reforms, but he has done no more than hint at this. In general it is hardly to be wondered that Bushman, like Bailyn, was not prepared to think in terms of overcrowding and increasing stratification. [Kenneth A. Lockridge, "Land, Population and the Evolution of New England Society, 1630–1790," *Past and Present*, 39 (1968), 62–80, which considers the case for "overcrowding," was, needless to say, not available for either author to consider.]

The best study of the emergence *after* the American Revolution of a truly unique and highly diverse and individualistic American social character is T. Scott Miyakawa's, *Protestants and Pioneers: Individualism and Conformity on the American Frontier* (Chicago, Ill., 1964). It is "best" largely because it corrects a further deficiency of Bushman's book, namely a reluctance to emphasize the way in which the localistic, corporative, conservative impulse of the past was absorbed into the new behavior and values of the slowly opening society. Miyakawa shows with sensitivity how the impulse at the heart of utopian communalism endured through the Anglicized eighteenth century to become an inseparable part of the new American individual of the nineteenth century.

Also useful are: Bernard Bailyn, *Education in the Forming of American Society* (New York, 1960); George Bancroft, *History of the United States* (10 vols., Boston, Mass., 1834–1874); Viola Barnes, *The Dominion of New England* (New Haven, Conn., 1923); Percy Wells Bidwell and John I. Falconer, *A History of Agriculture in the Northern United States, 1620–1860* (Washington, D.C., 1925); George A. Billias, *The Massachusetts Land Bankers of 1740* (Orono, Me., 1959); Elisha P. Douglass, *Rebels and Democrats:*

The Struggle for Equal Political Rights and Majority Rule during the American Revolution (Chapel Hill, N.C., 1955); Richard S. Dunn, *Puritans and Yankees: The Winthrop Dynasty of New England, 1603–1717* (Princeton, N.J., 1962); M. Eggleston, *The Land System of the New England Colonies* (Baltimore, Md., 1886); Zoltan Haraszti, *John Adams and the Prophets of Progress* (Cambridge, Mass., 1952); George D. Langdon, Jr., *Pilgrim Colony: A History of New Plymouth, 1620–1691* (New Haven, Conn., 1966); James Lemon, "Household Consumption in Eighteenth-Century America. . . ," *Agricultural History*, XLI (1967), 59–70; Richard B. Morris, *Studies in the History of American Law* (New York, 1930); Robert V. Remini, *The Election of Andrew Jackson* (New York, 1963); James Savage, *A Genealogical Dictionary of the First Settlers of New England* (4 vols., Boston, 1860–1862), which shall stand as a symbol of all the genealogical works consulted; James M. Smith, *Freedom's Fetters: The Alien and Sedition Laws and American Civil Liberties* (Ithaca, N.Y., 1956); Robert J. Taylor, *Western Massachusetts in the Revolution* (Providence, R.I., 1954); Frederick Jackson Turner, *The Frontier in American History* (New York, 1920); John William Ward, *Andrew Jackson: Symbol for an Age* (New York, 1955); and William B. Weeden, *Economic and Social History of New England, 1620–1789* (2 vols., Boston, Mass., 1891).

SECONDARY WORKS: BACKGROUND:
VILLAGE SOCIETY IN THE NON-WESTERN WORLD-EUROPE-ENGLAND

Equally important to an understanding of the New England Town is a knowledge of the characteristics of village society elsewhere in the world.

Peasants by Eric Wolf (Englewood Cliffs, N.J., 1966) is the only work on this universal subject that is clear and bold enough to be of value to an historian. Wolf's generalizations may offend some anthropologists, but his reputation in the profession is strong, he bases his ideas upon a profusion of case studies from all over the world, and those ideas do crystallize present knowledge of early New England towns into new insights. Wolf's "Closed Corporate Peasant Communities in Mesoamerica and Central Java," *Southwestern Journal of Anthropology*, XIII (Spring, 1957), 1–18, will supply more detail on his theories, especially on the dilemma of disintegration which faces such communities. For a related theoretical work on the development of social stratification, see Morton H. Fried, "On the Evolution of Social Stratification and the State," in S. Diamond, ed., *Culture in History* (New York 1960).

E. Hobsbawm's "The Crisis of the Seventeenth Century," *Past and Present,* 5 and 6 (1954) offers a synthetic view of the political and organizational evolution of the European states in the early modern era, and in the process makes reference to population trends. But it is the terminology of Emile Lousse, *La Société d'Ancien Régime: Organizations et Representation Corporatives* (Paris, 1943), which, through Sydney James' "Colonial Rhode Island and the Beginnings of the Liberal, Rationalized State" has entered this book. Lousse posited a shift from corporate to hierarchical regimes of authority in early modern Europe. Building on Lousse, James depicts a similar shift shortly thereafter in Rhode Island. (It is in this sense that James' work implies that in at least part of colonial America the process of change was in some respects a process of Europeanization.)

Among the most suggestive studies on the origins and ideals of very early European peasant communities are Hans Lietzmann, *The Beginnings of the Christian Church* (trans. B. L. Woolf, London, 1937), and F. Graus, "Social Utopias in the Middle Ages," *Past and Present,* 38 (Dec., 1967), 3–19.

Susan Tax Freeman, "Religious Aspects of the Social Organization of a Castillian Village," (*American Anthropologist,* 1969) presents a contemporary village in Catholic Spain, and derives from it hypotheses applicable to the evolution of early New England towns. *Calvin's Geneva,* by E. William Monter (New York, 1967) and "Protestant Dogma and City Government: The Case of Nuremburg," *Past and Present,* 36 (1967), 38–58, by Gerald Strauss, uncover the workings of Protestant communalism in northern Europe in the early modern era.

Since French historians have led the way in developing sophisticated techniques of local analysis, many excellent works on the history of French towns and villages could be mentioned. The best among these are still Louis Henry and Etienne Gautier, *La Population de Crulai, Paroisse Normande* (Paris, 1958), and Pierre Goubert's incomparable *Beauvais et les Beauvaisis de 1600 à 1730* (Paris, 1958). For those who do not read French, Goubert's "The French Peasantry of the Seventeenth Century: A Regional Example," *Past and Present,* 10 (1956), 55–77, will at least outline his main concerns. With Marc Bloch, *Les Caractères Originaux de l'Histoire Rurale Française* (2 vols., Paris, 1952, 1956), these works leave no doubt that American rural society never approached the conditions of deprivation that could exist in large parts of France. Yet, when read with the studies of New England towns listed below, they make it equally evident that there were many similarities between American and French villages of the seventeenth and eighteenth centuries. Chief among these were demographic similarities. Since demography is so important in this context, and since the mode of analysis known as historical demography was virtually invented by the French, it might be well to include here *Des Registres Parroissiaux à l'Histoire de la Population* (Paris, 1958), by Louis Henry and Etienne Gautier—an exposition of some of the methods of historical demography applied in France.

An inquiry into the English rural background could begin with George C. Homans' *English Villagers of the Thirteenth Century* (Cambridge, Mass., 1941). But most of the available literature concentrates around the seventeenth century; which is to some degree fortunate, since this is the rural England from which the New England Town emerged.

W. G. Hoskins, *The Midland Peasant: The Economic and Social Structure of a Leicestershire Village* (London, 1957) is a well-rounded study of a single village in the sixteenth and seventeenth centuries, and is especially useful in that it contradicts the image of the lord-and-tenant-ridden rural hellhole to which American historians are wont to compare the villages of early New England. Martha Jane Ellis, "Halifax Parish, 1558–1640" (Ph.D. dissertation, Radcliffe-Harvard University, 1958) adds further touches of reality to the image of English country life. The pity is that there are not many more such integrated studies to give us a sense of the totality of English rural existence in the Tudor-Stuart age (and for that matter to follow the evolution of that existence well into the eighteenth century). For until these are completed, the question of precisely what was unique about life in the villages of earliest America must remain open.

Of the merely suggestive works which will have to suffice until adequate local studies are available, Mildred Campbell's staple *The English Yeoman under Elizabeth and the Early Stuarts* (New Haven, Conn., 1952), H. J. Habakkuk's "English Landownership, 1680–1740," *Economic History Review*, XIV (1940), 14, and the chapters on English villages and towns in Sumner Chilton Powell's *Puritan Village: The Formation of a New England Town* (Middletown, Conn., 1963) do indicate that there were fundamental respects in which the English villager of the seventeenth and early eighteenth centuries was not as well off as his American cousin: the comfortable status of yeoman was not as widely held in England as in America, land was harder to come by, and the opportunity to move to new land and start a new and largely self-governing village hardly existed.

Yet as Hoskins' *Midland Peasant* and the case of Dedham demonstrate, the relative lack of advantages of the English villager can easily be exaggerated, while the realms of American advantage did not embrace the whole of life and were not immune to erosion. And, while the only final comparison will have to be based on a number of such integral, long-term studies of both English and American villages, some others of the suggestive works now available offer glimpses of English village life which indicate that for every difference implied or stressed in the works of Campbell, Habakkuk, and Powell, there was a fundamental similarity between the English and American rural existences of the seventeenth and early eighteenth centuries. If these are any measure, the comparison which will emerge once enough integral local studies are completed will be essentially the complex one implied by Hoskins' *Midland Peasant* and this study of Dedham. Old myths will fall, and the uniqueness of earliest America will have to be stated more cautiously than ever.

Take the field of historical demography, for example. The English have learned quickly from their French mentors this new aspect of local analysis, as is shown in the collection of essays edited by D. E. C. Eversley and D. V. Glass, *Population in History* (Chicago, Ill., 1965), and by the manual edited by E. A. Wrigley, *et al.*, *An Introduction to English Historical Demography* (London, 1966). Among their local demographic inquiries have been, A. Drake, "An Elementary Exercise in Parish Register Demography," *Economic History Review*, XIV (1962), 427; and Peter Laslett and John Harrison, "Clayworth and Cogenhoe," in *Historical Essays, 1660–1750, Presented to David Ogg*, ed. H. E. Bell and R. L. Ollard (London, 1963), which Laslett followed up with his sensitive but unavoidably vague *The World We Have Lost* (London, 1965). From these studies and from studies of the demographic experience of Dedham and of other American villages, cited below, it becomes clear that the essential rhythms of life could well have been the same in the England and in the America of the seventeenth century; birth rates, death rates, marriage ages, and mobility rates apparently differed little in the two environments. It is too early to tell how far we may generalize from such demographic similarities to a broad similarity of the material conditions of life, but certainly the evidence points toward this generalization. It must be admitted that the conditions of life in America were usually sufficiently good to ensure a growing population, and that this was not always the case in England, as J. D. Chambers' *The Vale of Trent, 1670–1800* (London, 1957) demonstrates. Yet this advantage was seemingly not the result of dramatic differences in the material opportunities of the societies, but rather of small differences operating over long periods.

Likewise read in the context of Dedham's experience and of other New England local studies cited below, the work of Sidney and Beatrice Webb of *English Local Government . . .*, I, *The Parish and the County* (New York, 1906) points up another specific similarity between rural England and rural America. For all America's vaunted liberty, local government operated there largely as it operated in England. The legal framework of the New England town differed little from that of the English parish, and the operational oscillations of the parish between the poles of oligarchy and democracy were reproduced in New England, albeit sometimes from different causes.

So in speaking of the seventeenth and early eighteenth centuries, while there is a lack of suitable evidence, enough evidence does exist to suggest that Anglo-American differences have been exaggerated and that there were many specific similarities between the two societies. As far as the middle and later eighteenth century is concerned, however, there are so few works on rural society on either side of the Atlantic that precise judgments on Anglo-American similarities and differences will simply have to be suspended. In this instance claims of essential similarity and claims of essential difference must be given equal consideration until more is known.

SECONDARY WORKS: THE NEW ENGLAND TOWN

Case studies of New England towns should be read in the light of the historical literature concerning New England at large and concerning village society elsewhere in the world. Innocence of approach has its advantages, but not on this occasion, especially since many of the most recent case studies presume some knowledge of this extensive background.

Page Smith, *As a City upon a Hill: The Town in American*

History (New York, 1966) is the only synthetic work on its immense subject, and contains a fine bibliography of books on American towns from the seventeenth century to the twentieth. As the book progresses, Smith's fascinating ideas become increasingly flawed, but his generally conservative interpretation of the influence of the small town on American history and his stress on the model provided by the "covenanted communities" of early New England have lent vital confirmation to this author's interpretation of the history of Dedham.

The institutional history of the early New England town is covered admirably in *Early New England Towns: A Comparative Study of Their Development* (New York, 1908), by Anne Bush McLear, and less adequately but in a broader perspective by John F. Sly, *Town Government in Massachusetts* (Cambridge, Mass., 1930).

Though, in *Puritan Village*, Sumner Chilton Powell gave a balanced and induplicable account of the changes which emigration to New England brought to the lives of the Englishmen who settled Sudbury, Massachusetts, in the 1640's, he won a measure of popularity among general readers because in his conclusion he threw balance to the winds and repeated the myth that Americans want to hear. That very arrival in America was enough to transform human existence, to free men of the medieval shackles of European society and set them on the road to Jeffersonianism. One has only to read the text of Powell's book to see the inadequacy of this conception. Further, many other studies of early New England towns suggest a more cautious view: to wit, A. N. Garvan, *Architecture and Town Planning in Colonial Connecticut* (New Haven, Conn., 1951); William Haller, Jr., *The Puritan Frontier: Town-Planting in New England Colonial Development, 1630–1660* (New York, 1951); Leonard W. Labaree, *Milford, Connecticut: The Early Development of a Town as Shown in Its Land Records* (Connecticut Tercentenary Pamphlet, New Haven, Conn., 1933); John Coolidge, "Hingham Builds a Meetinghouse," *New England Quarterly,* XXIV (1961); 435–61; Philip Greven, Jr., "Old Patterns in the New World: The Distribution of Land in 17th Century Andover," *Essex Institute Historical Collections,* CI (1965), 133–48, "Family Structure in Seventeenth-Century Andover, Massachusetts," *William and Mary Quarterly,* XXIII (1966), 234–56, and "Four Generations: A Study of Family Structure, Inheritance, and Mobility in Andover, Massachusetts, 1630–1750" (Ph.D. dissertation, Harvard University, 1965); Kenneth A. Lockridge and

Alan Kreider, "The Evolution of Massachusetts Town Government, 1640 to 1740," *William and Mary Quarterly,* XXIII (1966), 549–74; on Dedham alone see Kenneth A. Lockridge, "The History of a Puritan Church," *New England Quarterly,* XL (1967), 399–424, and "The Population of Dedham, Massachusetts, 1636–1736," *Economic History Review,* XIX (1966), 318–44; and finally, John J. Waters' recent "Hingham, Massachusetts, 1631–1661: An East Anglian Oligarchy in the New World," *Journal of Social History,* I (1967–68), 352–70. All of these bring out the existence and in some cases the persistence of the English, the European, indeed the peasant past in the New World villages—a persistence brought on as much by a conscious popular attachment to the social patterns of the past as by fundamental similarities in the conditions of life in America and England or by that blind inertia which always preserves the past. Some of them reveal how remarkably long the patterns of the past endured despite all the temptations of America. In several cases there is an implicit suggestion that the social ideology of Puritan Christianity intensified the enduring attachment to certain of the ways of the past.

An extensive if not great debate has raged over the nature of the political system in these seventeenth-century towns. James Truslow Adams, *The Founding of New England* (Boston, Mass., 1921), saw Puritan New England as a repressive oligarchy, and claimed that at best one townsman in five met the requirement of church membership that enabled men to vote in colonial elections. B. Katherine Brown raised the level of discussion with her articles, "Freemanship in Puritan Massachusetts," *American Historical Review,* LIX (1954), 865–83, and "A Note on the Puritan Concept of Aristocracy," *Mississippi Valley Historical Review,* XLI (1954–55), 105–12. With these supplying theoretical and legal background, she has gone on to investigate the level of colonial and local suffrage, the operation of that suffrage in making local decisions, and the nature of local leadership, in the towns of Cambridge and Dedham: as witness "Puritan Democracy: A Case Study," *Mississippi Valley Historical Review,* L (1963–1964), 396; and "Puritan Democracy in Dedham, Massachusetts: Another Case Study," *William and Mary Quarterly,* XXIV (1967), 396. Mrs. Brown has established that the suffrage in New England towns was probably never as low as twenty percent, that the local leadership was never a repressive oligarchy limited to the most wealthy saints, and that there were elements in the Puritan ideology and influences in the American environment which encouraged wide popular participation in politics.

But in the opinion of this author, Mrs. Brown has gone too far along the line of argument already excessively applied to the eighteenth-century colonies by her husband (Robert E. Brown, *Middle-Class Democracy and the Revolution in Massachusetts*). She has repeatedly invoked the bare labels, "democracy," in describing seventeenth-century New England in general and its towns in particular. She seems to have based this invocation primarily upon her assertion that more than eighty percent of adult males could vote both in colonial and in local elections, but also to some degree upon a less than perfect understanding of Puritan ideology and of the suffrage laws which grew out of that ideology. Growing numbers of historians have sought to correct her image of early New England politics with a portrayal of the subject centered somewhere between Adam's "oligarchy" and her rarely qualified "democracy." The efforts of Robert E. Wall, Jr., "A New Look at Cambridge," *Journal of American History,* LII (1965–66), 599–605; J. R. Pole, "Historians and the Problem of Early American Democracy," *American Historical Review,* LXVII (1961–62), 626–46; John M. Murrin, "The Myths of Colonial Democracy and Royal Decline in Eighteenth-Century America," *Cithara,* V (1965), 53–60, have been primarily critical, and Pole and Murrin have directed their comments as much to the eighteenth as to the seventeenth-century applications of the Brown thesis. Other efforts have concentrated on adding evidence, though in many cases the authors have expressed or implied criticisms of Mrs. Brown's view: see Richard C. Simmons, "Studies in the Massachusetts Franchise, 1631–1691," (Ph.D. dissertation, University of California, Berkeley, 1965), "Freemanship in Early Massachusetts: Some Suggestions and a Case Study," *William and Mary Quarterly,* XIX (1962), 422–28, and the forthcoming "Godliness, Property, and the Massachusetts Franchise," *Journal of American History,* 1968; also, Kenneth A. Lockridge and Alan Kreider, "The Evolution of Massachusetts Town Government"; and Stephen Foster, "The Massachusetts Franchise in the Seventeenth Century," *William and Mary Quarterly,* XXIV (1967), 613–23. Also relevant are David H. Fowler, "Connecticut's Freeman: The First Forty Years," *William and Mary Quarterly,* XV (1958), 312–33, and George D. Langdon, Jr., "The Franchise and Political Democracy in Plymouth Colony," *ibid.,* XX (1963), 513–26; and John Waters' piece on "Hingham . . . 1631–1661: An East Anglian Oligarchy in the New World."

What does it all come to? For one thing, in finding in Mrs. Brown's presentations of Puritan literature, laws, and political practices specific errors and omissions (and in some cases by having her find similar shortcomings in their work) historians have discovered that the subject is more difficult to study than had been expected. Puritan political theory is supremely ambiguous, the suffrage laws are not well understood, and studies of the local suffrage and of local political practices demand more sophisticated techniques of analysis and better demographic information than have yet been employed. Despite these problems, a sort of consensus on the substance of early Massachusetts politics is emerging. While both Puritan political theory and English village practices put a high value on popular participation, both in theory and in practice there were strong countervailing emphases on peace, order, and consensual unity which were antithetical to "democracy" in today's sense of a society of equal individuals possessing both the freedom and the power to dissent. The suffrage laws put these conservative influences into practice by restricting the suffrage to the saints of the church and/or to the relatively wealthy: in short, by limiting participation to men who were expected to have the interests of peace, unity, and order foremost in their minds at polling time. At first, to be sure, these laws permitted from sixty to eighty percent of adult males to vote for colonial officers, and from sixty to ninety percent to vote in town elections. But by the 1680's these figures had fallen to around thirty to sixty percent and forty to seventy percent, respectively, as a result of declining church membership and increased property requirements for the local suffrage. It may be that by this time in most towns a majority of men held no suffrage whatsoever. Moreover, even in the period of high suffrage, townsmen had used their votes to elect repeatedly a few, relatively wealthy leaders. They had rarely questioned the decisions of that leadership. So, all in all, while hardly an out-and-out oligarchy, this system was no "democracy" in any sense familiar to Americans today. Only with a string of qualifying adjectives can that word be applied to early Massachusetts. As B. Katherine Brown seems now to agree, when she says, "I have always maintained that the Bay Colony was not democratic in its relations with the world community. But in its internal structure my evidence indicates that early Massachusetts had much more democracy than it has been credited with in the past, call it what you will." [*William and Mary Quarterly*, XXV (1968), 339.] Most of her critics will settle for this, though most would prefer a more precise description of this unique and subtly conservative political system.

As any resident of the Hub knows, Boston is unique. Its development was so accelerated that it soon passed out of the realm of the New England Town to become the first New England city. But its rapid development in the seventeenth century does serve to foreshadow the changes that would strike many New England towns in the eighteenth; as can be seen from Darrett Rutman's rich and imaginative *Winthrop's Boston,* (Chapel Hill, N.C., 1965) and James A. Henretta's "Economic Development and Social Structure in Colonial Boston," *William and Mary Quarterly,* XXII (1965), 75–92. Rutman's "The Mirror of Puritan Authority," in George A. Billias, ed., *Law and Authority in Colonial America: Selected Essays* (Barre, Mass., 1965) reflects to some extent the pecularities of an urbanizing Boston—and Sumner Powell's whiggish interpretation of early Sudbury—in its conclusion that in the mid-seventeenth century "the man in the village lane" was not greatly affected by Puritan social ideology. A close look at evidence old and new from other villages of the time, or for that matter at the evidence from Sudbury, might have revealed that this admittedly fascinating conclusion was perhaps a bit premature.

Students of the earliest New England towns might also wish to consult: Charles M. Andrews, *The River Towns of Connecticut* (Baltimore, Md., 1889); Charles F. Adams, *The Genesis of the Massachusetts Town* (Cambridge, Mass., 1892), and *Three Episodes of Massachusetts History* (Boston, Mass., 1892); Herbert B. Adams, "The Germanic Origin of New England Towns," *Johns Hopkins University; Studies in Historical and Political Science,* I (Baltimore, Md., 1882), 5–38; John Demos, "Notes on Life in Plymouth Colony," *William and Mary Quarterly,* XXII (1965), 264–86; Frank Smith, *A History of Dedham, Massachusetts* (Dedham, Mass., 1936); and the *Dedham Historical Register* (14 vols., Dedham, Mass., 1890–1904).

As for the changes that came with time, the quiet process of largely spiritual "decline" which weakened the Puritan social synthesis in the towns of the middle and later seventeenth century is treated in the works by Haller, Simmons, Langdon, and Lockridge and Kreider, already cited. Gillian Lindt Gollin, *Moravians in Two Worlds* (New York, 1965) offers a comparative approach to a similar process in colonial Pennsylvania.

The story of the somewhat more dramatic and certainly more material changes that took place within Dedham in the eighteenth century will be found in the articles by Lockridge, already cited. These must be supplemented by Edward M. Cook, Jr., "The Transformation of Dedham, Massachusetts, 1715–1750 (Senior Honors Thesis, Harvard University, 1965), and "Social Behavior and

Changing Values in Dedham, Massachusetts, 1700–1775" (unpublished article manuscript, 1968).

As for other towns in the eighteenth century, there *is* evidence
of similar changes, although it is as yet a bit ambiguous or limited.
The best and very nearly the only comprehensive study of New
England towns in the first half of the eighteenth century is Michael
Zuckerman, "The Massachusetts Town in the Eighteenth Century"
(Ph.D. dissertation, Harvard University, 1967). This work contains much evidence of a process of conflict and diversification
which was leading to new modes of behavior somewhat like those
depicted in the case of Dedham and in Richard Bushman's study
of Connecticut (*Puritan to Yankee*). Zuckerman prefers to emphasize instead the tranquillity of his rural societies as compared
with modern America and to stress the persistence of the communal
ideology inherited from the past; but, while this outlook is deeply
perceptive, he emphasizes it to the point of seeming to ignore the
possibility raised by his own evidence that a hundred and more
years of history might have done *something* to disturb the communal
equilibrium established in the seventeenth century. Both Charles S.
Grant's *Democracy in the Connecticut Frontier Town of Kent*
(New York, 1961), a valued but still grossly underrated book, and
"Religion, Finance, and Democracy in Massachusetts: the Town
of Norton as a Case Study" (paper delivered at the Iowa University
Conference on Early American History, March, 1967) by John M.
Bumsted, implicitly support this author's and Bushman's portrait
of an "opening" of society in the eighteenth-century towns, yet
they also qualify that portrait. Their qualification is that a trend
to overcrowding quite like that in Dedham shut out opportunity
shortly after the "opening" had increased individual liberty. This
is as valid as the qualification entered by Zuckerman and has the
virtue of being more moderately stated.

Beyond these few works and the latter chapters of Philip
Greven's apparently excellent dissertation on Andover the literature
of the New England town in the eighteenth century is sparse. Some
information may be gotten from Richard Le Baron Bowen, *Early
Rehoboth* (4 vols., Rehoboth, Mass., 1945–1950), indirectly from
Ola Winslow, *Meetinghouse Hill* (New York, 1952), and from
such local works as George Cooke's *History of Clapboard
Trees, or Third Parish* (Boston, Mass., 1887), George Clarke's
History of Needham (Cambridge, Mass., 1912), Willard DeLue's
Story of Walpole (Norwood, 1925), or Frank Smith's *History of
Dover* (Boston, Mass., 1896). Carlos P. Slafter, *A Record of*

Education, The Schools and Teachers of Dedham . . . 1644–1904
(Dedham, Mass., 1905) is helpful for Dedham, but has few
counterparts in other towns.

Anyone venturing to study the nineteenth century should see
Benjamin W. Labaree, *Patriots and Partisans: The Merchants of
Newburyport, 1764–1815* (Cambridge, Mass., 1962), and Stephen
Thernstrom, *Poverty and Progress: Social Mobility in a Nineteenth
Century City* (Cambridge, Mass., 1964), which also deals interest-
ingly with Newburyport, Massachusetts, and does so with superb
method (if with an almost uselessly small sample of its society).
Interesting as these are, they are far from sufficient to describe the
critical transition that faced the towns of Massachusetts as they
moved from the Anglo-Americanism of 1763 to and beyond the
America of de Tocqueville and the 1830's.

DOCUMENTARY SOURCES: DEDHAM

The sources used to recreate the history of Dedham are by
and large the same sources that exist for the history of any New
England town. For a more complete account of the potential
sources for the history of any and all such towns, however, see the
bibliography in Michael Zuckerman's dissertation.

The Town records are the staple item, in this case published
as *Early Records of the Town of Dedham* (6 vols., 1886–1936),
ed., Don Gleason Hill (I–V), and Julius H. Tuttle (VI). Volumes
III–VI include run-of-the-mill town business, elections, special
petitions, and tax lists. The tax lists and the vital records (births,
marriages, deaths, *Records* I) must be used with the utmost care,
but so used they can be employed in tandem to uncover as much
about the society as all other local records combined. The church
records (*Records,* II) give data on membership and discipline.
Because of the historical consciousness of Dedham's first minister,
they also describe the founding of the church in great detail.

Manuscript town records and land records in the Town Hall,
together with miscellaneous deeds, letters, and diaries in the Dedham Historical Society, supplement the published records.

On the county level, the Suffolk County Probate, Court, and
Registry of Deeds records in the Courthouse in Boston are most
useful. Some warnings are necessary, however. The wills and
inventories, which so thoroughly describe the families, aspirations,
and possessions of the townsmen, are not complete; they exist for,

and so describe, a minority or at best a narrow majority of men. The Court records are scattered; the myriad *Files* in the possession of the Supreme Court are so full as to be almost impossible to use, while the Common Pleas and other transcripts of proceedings in court are in the possession of agents of the modern Superior Court who often cannot find them. The Deeds are incomplete for the seventeenth century, probably because men were careless about registering land transactions.

The Massachusetts Archives in the basement of the State House are *the* source for any events involving Dedham's relation to colonial authorities. But since the Archives are largely un-catalogued, it is anyone's guess what they contain. Only by judicious sampling of microfilm versions made available on the spot by the very able Leo Flaherty, by use of the few catalogued volumes, and by recourse to published sources that duplicate some of the material in the Archives, can this level of information be made to yield a decent return.

The letters and documents in the Massachusetts Historical Society are fairly well catalogued. Sometimes they provide the explicit information that confirms an event or trend deduced only indirectly from the cryptic town records.

Both the Massachusetts Historical Society and Harvard's Houghton Library have collections of contemporary publications. The Houghton Library has John Allin's *Defence of the Nine Positions* (London, 1648, with Thomas Shepard) and his elegantly titled *Animadversions on the Antisynodalia Americana* (Cambridge, Mass., 1664).

Published sources make research much more convenient. Herman Mann, *Historical Annals of Dedham* (Dedham, Mass., 1847) reprints and synopsizes some local manuscript records. The *Watertown Records* (4 vols., Watertown, Mass., 1894 and 1900; Boston, Mass., 1904 and 1906) describe life in a neighboring town. The Records of the Suffolk County Court, 1671–1680, are in the *Publications of the Colonial Society of Massachusetts*, XXX (2 vols., Boston, 1933), which saves some research in the courthouse. *The Records of the Court of Assistants of the Colony of Massachusetts Bay, 1630–1692* (3 vols., Boston, Mass., 1904), are both judicial and legislative in nature. The legislative acts of the colony can also be followed in William H. Whitmore, ed., *A Bibliographical Sketch of the Laws of the Massachusetts Bay Colony . . . 1630 to 1686* (Boston, Mass., 1890). For the provincial period, the equivalents are the *Journal of the House of Representatives of Massa-*

chusetts Bay (Boston, Mass., 1919–1965), and the *Acts and Resolves . . . of the Province of Massachusetts Bay . . . .* (Boston, 1869–1922).

Other published sources include E. Burgess, *Dedham Pulpit* (Boston, Mass., 1840); Perry Miller and Thomas H. Johnson, eds., *The Puritans* (2 vols., New York, 1963); Edward Johnson's *Wonder-Working Providence of Sion's Saviour in New England,* ed., J. F. Jameson (New York, 1910); and items in the *New England Historic-Genealogical Register* (Boston, Mass., 1880–   ). Glimpses of political and constitutional thought in late eighteenth-century Dedham and in other Massachusetts towns can be found in the definitive *The Popular Sources of Political Authority: Documents on the Massachusetts Constitution of 1780,* edited and with an introduction by Oscar and Mary Handlin (Cambridge, Mass., 1966); some of the same documents are more readily available in Robert Taylor, *Massachusetts, Colony to Commonwealth: Documents on the Formation of Its Constitution, 1775–1780* (Chapel Hill, N.C., 1961). The latter is in some ways the more perceptive book, and its selections will suffice to show that many elements of the old communalistic ideology survived in the towns of Massachusetts long after the "utopian" age had passed.

Index